Female Ambition

Female Ambition

How to Reconcile Work and Family

Nuria Chinchilla

and

Consuelo León

First published 2005 by
PALGRAVE MACMILLAN
Houndmills, Basingstoke, Hampshire RG21 6XS and
175 Fifth Avenue, New York, N.Y. 10010
Companies and representatives throughout the world

PALGRAVE MACMILLAN is the global academic imprint of the Palgrave
Macmillan division of St. Martin's Press, LLC and of Palgrave Macmillan Ltd.
Macmillan® is a registered trademark in the United States, United Kingdom
and other countries. Palgrave is a registered trademark in the European
Union and other countries.

ISBN-13: 978–1–4039–9178–2
ISBN-10: 1–4039–9178–2

This book is printed on paper suitable for recycling and made from fully
managed and sustained forest sources.

A catalogue record for this book is available from the British Library.

Library of Congress Cataloging-in-Publication Data
Chinchilla Albiol, Ma. Nuria (María Nuria)
[Ambición femenia. English]
Female ambition : how to reconcile work and family / by Nuria Chinchilla
and Consuelo León.
     p.   cm.
Includes bibliographical references and index.
ISBN 1–4039–9178–2 (cloth)
1. Work and family.   2. Working mothers.   3. Women in the
professions.   I. León, Consuelo.   II. Title.
HD4904.25.C4613 2005
331.4′4—dc22   2005049815

10   9   8   7   6   5   4   3   2   1
14   13   12   11   10   09   08   07   06   05

Printed and bound in Great Britain by
Antony Rowe Ltd, Chippenham and Eastbourne

To you, women, who struggle to be an agent of change
To you, men, who believe in women and share this ambition

Contents

List of Tables

Foreword

In a world where both the nature of work and the character of the work force are rapidly changing, points of tension are likely to arise. Among the key ones are the tensions between work and family and between men's and women's roles. These tensions are poignantly described in this book. Their effects are exacerbated in Spain, where temporal norms create overlong work days interrupted by long, food-laden lunch breaks. They show up in low birth rates, failures of children in school, a high divorce rate, and low productivity.

Though the descriptions in this book come from Spanish managers, the issues discussed transcend nationality. Indeed, they occur, though in somewhat different form, in the whole industrialized world. Business is becoming more competitive, more global. Everywhere people are being asked to do more; workloads, particularly of managers, are increasing. And, for both psychological and economic reasons, more and more women are entering the work force. We are left, therefore, with significant deficits in care, and run the risk of not socializing the youngest generation to the responsibilities they will have to undertake as they reach maturity. It is this dilemma, this warning about the future, that is detailed in this book.

The model being used is 'female ambition' – an ambition geared to success in all facets of life, not just in the occupational world. It is based on a notion of complementarities between men and women and among work, family, community and self. It recognizes that there are skills learned in the family that could significantly enhance business in today's world, that time for reflection is critical for creativity and to prevent burnout, and that current work practices make it difficult to enact these truths. Based on existing literature, the words of scholars throughout the ages, as well as on the concrete experiences of a group of managers, this book paints a moving picture of both the difficulties and the possibilities of leading harmonious lives.

Government and community obviously play a role – in support of care most immediately, but also in a more general assessment of mismatches, such as reconciling school hours with work hours. Our school calendar is still based on an agrarian model, even as the work has moved to an industrial and post-industrial base.

Employers, too, must become aware of the advantages to them of having employees whose lives encompass more than their employment – who can bring interpersonal skills, reflective creativity and energy to their employment. *Female Ambition* outlines a telling set of indicators that should alert employers and employees to problems: for example, talking only about work at company social events, having too many meetings, expecting continuous accessibility, realizing that going to the movies or the theatre is an exceptional event. Every company and every worker could usefully inspect this list and ponder their own situations.

All of this is important, but difficult for any individual to control. So in the end the emphasis is on personal leadership. We need to take control of our lives, develop interpersonal intelligence, and use the freedoms we have to be proactive about our situations. We need to remember that human needs span the material, the cognitive and the affective worlds. We need to be mature in all and not emphasize one to the neglect of the others. Only then can subjective success be achieved, and that is what determines life satisfaction – more than any external markers of fame. We all know stories of people seemingly extremely successful who are never satisfied and deeply unhappy.

This is the message that comes through this book. It comes in multiple forms: in the language of values and received thought, and in very practical terms of how to deal with life on a day-to-day basis. Keep a diary! But include in it not only personal affairs, and not only work details, but both – in the same diary. It is this complementariness that is the essence of female ambition, and it applies to men as well as women. It provides the basis for a successful life and a successful society.

LOTTE BAILYN
T. Wilson Professor of Management
Co-Director, MIT Workplace Center
Sloan School of Management
Massachusetts Institute of Technology
Cambridge, MA

Preface

It is often said that work and family reconciliation policies will be the most significant social policies to emerge from the 21st century. In the face of the many challenges faced by society – globalization, the shifting labour market and new technologies – successful leaders will be those who can provide effective answers and alternatives in this new era.

But today's consumers and voters are currently facing an uphill battle in their struggle to reconcile work and family life – a situation that presents a potent source of conflict for all of society. The urgent need to find ways to integrate professional lives with families is an issue that penetrates discussions around the world, political platforms, novels and TV shows, as well as new policies being developed by human resources managers within companies.

In recent years the world has been concerned with protecting our *external ecosystem*, our environmental resources, in order to preserve the ecological balance of the planet. Thus, we have implemented laws to encourage companies to be respectful and act responsibly towards the environment. Now the focus of governments and companies has turned toward the *internal ecosystem* of our world, the work/life balance of people and families. The topic of quality of life now includes concepts such as balance, harmony, flexibility, working by objectives and quality time – in short, how men and women can work and live together in a shared world.

Research at the International Center for Work and Family (ICWF) at IESE Business School of the University of Navarra, http://www.iese.edu/icwf, seeks to provide insights on this critical topic. Our work is supported by the Dean of the school, Professor Jordi Canals, who believes in the strategic importance of the Center's initiatives, as well as the faculty members at IESE, particularly Professors Steven Poelmans, Pablo Cardona, Miguel Angel Ariño, José María Rodríguez, Lorenzo Dionis and Juan Carlos Vázquez-Dodero. The work of deceased Professor Juan Antonio Pérez López, also contributes to the center, since we draw upon his humanistic vision of management action as the solid foundation for our work. Larisa Tatge of IESE's Publications Department also assisted with the publication of this book.

We would also like to thank the European Union, the Spanish government and the country's regional governments, the alumni of IESE Business School, the companies that sponsor the ICWF, the Center's researchers and assistants, as well as our families, who have given us their support, trust and collaboration to make this book a reality.

NURIA CHINCHILLA
CONSUELO LEÓN

Introduction

'Women who seek to be equal to men lack ambition.'

Timothy Leary

The reconciliation of working and family life, the specific contribution of women to companies, their role as agents of change, the styles of female and male management are all subjects that are present throughout this book joined by a common thread: female ambition. Women in the 21st century want to be mothers, wives, professionals, citizens... all at the same time, and there is no turning back on this process.

What do women think about? The press, public opinion and even some literature arising from certain media sometimes give the idea that we women have gone mad and only think about demanding rights and waving flags.

We go to the gymnasium, we scream in traffic jams, and we put up with separations, divorces, disputes, romances, two-shift working days and even power races, but our true ambition is to have a full life that can be called so.

In the post-yuppie era and in light of such serious workplace problems as addiction to work and the 'burn-out' syndrome, what truly concerns women is to feel that they have support in designing their own working life outside the traditional male lines (which ignore mother-hood) and to see that governments are taking measures along these lines by legislating and giving direct, effective aid.

In the new context of this silent revolution in ordinary life, women want their femininity to be respected and to be given the

1

opportunity to show that their specific contribution is capable of transforming companies and society to make them more welcoming and more humane. And what do they need to do this? The complicity and co-operation of men, and confidence, a great deal of confidence that things will work despite having to change . . . a lot.

We women want the freedom to be able to put 'married and mother of two' on our CVs; to get pregnant or say we are going to do so soon; to be recognized as something more than a qualified workforce that is interesting, efficient and complementary to men. In short, we aspire to not only not hide our family, but make it compatible with our professional work. At the same time, we do not want this to be the result of a private battle, but rather the recognition of a social right.

We women think, or rather dream, of politicians, businessmen and social agents who take a chance on the fixed return value, albeit long term, of motherhood. That they or we might envision solutions and ways to reduce the 'cost' (it is sad to say it this way) of the children that a woman might have throughout her working life. Let us use imagination, let us avoid what is facile. Let us take a chance on a true welfare society, based on its components being able to think and exist well.

Although it is true that everything is changing, not everything has been resolved. When we thought about writing this book, we were not only replying to the momentum this topic has generated in public opinion, we wanted also to serve as a platform for social dialogue in the passionate crusade of seeking alternative solutions and ways, since the goal is to foster a legal, public and working context that facilitates freedom of choice. We must bear in mind that today, 60 per cent of women have ambitions to make two things, work and family,[1] compatible. Another 20 per cent opt exclusively for their families and the remaining 20 per cent for their careers. The changes in our society will necessarily follow these lines: to assure the context of freedom so that every family and every woman can choose.

The family is the greatest existing area where everything important is free. Here people are loved and accepted just for themselves at all times. The relationships are essentially affective, and although there is reciprocity, they are not motivated by self-interest. Although living together may be difficult at times, families tend to forgive, protect and care for their members even in circumstances in which the environment (work, friends and health) might fail. It is impossible to plan any similar type of social organization. Here each individual is loved and accepted simply because he or she exists. Our society lives on this basic core of civic guarantees and core value. We cannot merely look at the family with affection based on the fear of a society without pensions or the reversal of the population age pyramid. For the company too, as we shall show in these pages, the employees' family environment is key, since a large part of an individual's equilibrium, balance and habit-learning necessary for working life comes from this reality.

On the other hand, for all men (men and women), work is a source of self-realization and socialization. Work is serving and is, indeed, living. However, in the past thirty years, we have witnessed a celebration of paid work as the main indicator of a person's value. You are no longer worth what you have managed to be but what the market pays you. This purely economic view, in which the only things of value are those that can be quantified and paid, has influenced a progressive devaluation of household work. Regardless of whether a woman can or cannot devote more time to them, these tasks are deserving of enormous social and personal recognition, as the home is the public service par excellence, the best Ministry of Social Welfare and crime prevention centre. According to several studies, the value of unpaid household work done in Spain mainly by women, if paid at market value, would be equivalent to 40 per cent of the gross domestic product. Household work, so little appreciated at times in favour of work outside the home, fulfils an essential role not only because of its invisible yet real value in the gross domestic product, or because of the savings it means for public social services, but also because its very nature develops personal skills and competences related to service and co-existence. For this reason, men also benefit personally when they take part in the housework.

An agreement between two

If it were necessary to draw up a diagram of the situation of women throughout history, three phrases would suffice: the private area (family), public life (paid work, participation in political and social life) and, finally, rupture (women give their talents to the working world, but the working world does not provide flexibility). Today one of the great challenges facing individuals is to re-establish this harmony among individuals, companies and countries.

In our studies of dual-income families, that is, families in which both father and the mother work outside the home, it can be seen that although an individual's working environment is important, the greatest cause of conflict between work and family is each individual's way of handling the problem. Business culture, that is, a company's modus operandi and values, may facilitate or hamper reconciliation, but the resolution of the problem is something personal, unique and unrepeatable. It is a question of taking decisions according to personal priorities and anticipating situations of conflict. Every married couple has to agree on this part of their joint project (how to take care of the house and their respective jobs), just as they have to agree on the mortgage, the children's school and holidays.

Companies: a change of mentality

The time has come to consider every professional, who is at the same time a citizen, father or mother of a family, child, etc. This attitude is not only socially responsible, but in the long run it is more profitable for a company in order to gain the loyalty of its employees with something more than money: with trust translated into flexibility. In this context, management by objectives and not by hours of presence has become the most serious target in the labour problem in our country: 'eternal' working days that have no positive effect on greater productivity.

In Spain, people work too many hours; this is our national vice which is determined by a late, excessively long lunch at midday that extends the working day, which leads to a professional profile characterized by an addiction to work, which in turn leads to 'burn-out' syndrome, and its opposite, absenteeism, something that nobody hesitates to associate with disinterest and lack of commitment, but which maybe should be analysed more closely to determine how often it hides not enough time to get everything done. Stress is the greatest cause of sick leave in our country, and in the case of women, it is the main reason why they leave their careers.

This situation also diminishes motivation and creativity, two qualities that are very highly valued in companies, two intangible factors which can enormously increase the value of a team, of a company, and even more so in times such as the present when different solutions are required in the context of a global village and constant change.

At a time like now, when we already have a European currency and a European job market, why have we not yet got a European timetable?

The main asset, not only of the company but of the whole of society, is people. We have heard this no end of times, but maybe we still don't really believe it. Yet the most serious concern is that we are endangering 'human ecology'. For many decades companies showed no concern about their impact on the environment, but today this has changed. There are regulations, quality certifications, legislation and sanctions that have made companies more sensitive to their social responsibility with respect to the pollution generated in nature. However, it is true that many companies today systematically contaminate the human environment where they are and with which they work without being aware of it. When a worker is not allowed to play their role of husband or wife, or father or mother, or son or daughter, due to rigid or interminable timetables or constant travelling, they are being impoverished as a person, in addition to having their marital or parent–child relationship jeopardized.

If there is no time to enjoy the family, the number of children falls and homes are not made. The fact is that the abandonment or omission of families means that values are not conveyed, good habits are not developed and society is impoverished. Family, company and society are living realities that form a triangle in constant evolution which is enriched or devalued through individuals' positive learning in the different areas of their life. Seeing what is happening around us, are we not destroying this place of co-existence par excellence, which is the family?

The pollution of rivers is corrected in some cases by building fish factories, which have saved more than one aquatic species, but people are not developed as easily as animals, and if we do not allow the family to fulfil its function, what will the new 'human factory' be like? As the French writer André Frossard wrote, 'ancient civilisations were destroyed by the barbarian invasions; ours has the barbarians within it'.[2] We must therefore take care of the family if we do not wish to work against ourselves.

If we lose sight of this, if we stop giving importance to one of the main reasons behind the breakdown of marriages and educational problems within the family and schools; or if we look indifferently at the fact that many women managers (current or potential) self-impose a cement ceiling in their professional careers in order to avoid further conflict between their professional and family lives; if we consider as a secondary problem the fact that there are discriminatory measures in companies not only because of sex but also because of motherhood (let us not forget that a woman without family obligations – children, parents or dependents – is hardly ever a 'problem'), we are avoiding reality and its possible solutions.

This book starts with two chapters that describe the situation of women throughout history and the current situation of the family and government aid in different countries. Once the subject is framed within its context, we will go into the challenges caused by the inclusion of women in the workplace and how work and family often collide due to a lack of support from government, enterprise or civil society. Then we will examine good practices in each of these areas: personal, family, government and enterprise, stressing the fact that the family, despite everything, is a competitive advantage for individuals in all orders of life. Therefore, the different chapters of this work cover the unique contribution by women to the working world as a true agent of change – so necessary in today's companies – and they encourage us to reflect on personal leadership as a condition *sine qua non* for leading others. The last chapter gives us clues as how to effectively manage our multiple agendas.

Both authors, one as the Director of the Centre for Research into Work and Family and a teacher at IESE, and the other as a journalist and researcher at IESE, have made an in-depth study of this reality from different areas and viewpoints. In this book, we have compiled the results of our research with female managers, as these are the people who experience conflict more intensely (stress, long working days, being minorities) and at the same time who are in the privileged situation of being able to take decisions to generate the cultural change that is necessary and beneficial for everyone. In these pages, it is clear that many wish to accomplish this, but hand-in-hand with men, because society and family belong to both.

1
Being a Woman in the Twenty-first Century

'The past is a prologue.'

Shakespeare

'Tell me what you truly love and you will have given me an expression of your life.'
'You love what you live.'

J.G. Fitche

The history of women and feminism

Our times are undoubtedly *a time of women*.[1] There are three basic events that have taken place around the status of women in this century: the right to vote with its consequent legal autonomy with respect to civil rights; greater equality in access to education; and the massive entry of women in the job market.

Much has been written about this social change; however, the history leading up to it is as yet unwritten, when women did not appear in public, visible forums, when they played a role in events that are not mentioned by historical sources, and when they acted as family support, shaping the private life of peoples. They were also present at this time, but in a different way.

In feudal times (from the tenth to the thirteenth centuries), women in the upper classes were able to have and administer feuds, they participated in the Crusades and governed, and some even achieved high political, economic and social standing due to their position, lands, family or business.[2] This situation changed in later centuries and particularly in the modern, contemporary era with the development of the bourgeois mentality and the influence of the 1804 Napoleonic Code, which would be copied by other countries.[3]

Hegel justified the causes of this marginalization by claiming that men had to achieve in the service of the three prevailing social activities, namely science, state and economy, precisely those that Weber regarded as the heritage of Western civilization. Many Catholic feminist movements encountered difficulties in their struggle for universal suffrage, particularly in England. Perhaps the reason was that women represented a sector of conservative ideology. Was it necessary to grant them this right?

In the early 19th century, women did not vote or hold public positions, nor did they own property, as they transferred all inherited goods to their husbands. Of course, they were not allowed to trade or have their own businesses or exercise many professions, open current accounts or obtain credit. The civil and penal codes considered them minors before the law.

Women's suffrage was won throughout the 20th century: first in Australia (1901), Denmark (1905), Finland (1906), Norway (1913), Holland and Russia (1917), England and Germany (1918), Sweden (1919) and the United States (1920). It would be gained later in other European countries, for instance in Spain (1931), France and Italy (1945) and Switzerland (1975).[4]

Furthermore, women first entered universities in the United States and then in Europe. In 1837 the first women's college was opened, Mount Holyoke, in Massachusetts, and was followed by others. With respect to women's admission into men's universities, in Europe this was first allowed in England (Queen's, 1848) and it later spread to France (1880) and Germany (1894).

The massive influx of women into the job market (except for work in factories during the Industrial Revolution) had hardly started by the middle of the last century. It was precisely the impact of World War I that largely changed the course of history. Many women had to take the jobs that the men left to go to war. This was how they demonstrated their talent in sectors such as health care and education. It is hardly surprising that ever since that time, women have been the driving force behind specific activist movements involving politics and thinking, with broad repercussions in our culture and way of living.

Having achieved these advances, and immersed in what we might call a 'reformist feminism', there was a pause until the 1960s. In the Anglo-Saxon world, having achieved the main feminist demands (for the vote, access to higher education and divorce), many feminist groups disappeared or cut back their activities. In Spain, a noteworthy step was the modification of the civil code in 1958, in which the concept of 'the husband's house', defining the couple's common home, was replaced with the term 'marital home'. Before this date, since the husband was the exclusive administrator of their belongings, after a separation, in addition to losing their home, women were also left penniless. Following the reform (spearheaded by the writer and jurist, Mercedes Formica), women were able to have the use of the marital home following a separation.

Later, we witnessed a second wave of what we might call 'revolutionary feminism'. The existentialist philosopher Marcuse[5] recognized that this movement was the most significant, radical movement that existed at the time, Marxism included. Those were years when the number of women at university and in different jobs increased significantly. The radical protest movement reached its peak in support of Black civil rights in the United States, and the student revolts and the May turmoil of 1968 in France, with the hippie culture. In this context, a 'new ethics' was being advocated that would break with society and the conventional family, and which would 'free' women from the 'chains of nature', as Simone de Beauvoir termed it.[6] Her book *The Second Sex* was particularly influential in the United States; her thesis was that women are always 'the other' and are not 'born', but 'made' ('you're not born a feminist, you become a feminist' is the phrase she coined and which became her slogan). Since they are 'reduced to the world of the bodily' or at least this is understood, women must precisely be freed of their bodies. Many see in this deprecation of the bodily reality a reflection of the misogynous nature of her companion, the existentialist Jean-Paul Sartre.

What was changing? 'Until now, the revolutions had only been directed against human institutions: the French Revolution in 1789 abolished the class society; the Bolshevik Revolution in 1917 abolished the private means of production. Now the intention was to eliminate the consequences of the bipolar sexuality of the person'.[7] For many thinkers (the philosopher Julián Marías[8] and the psychiatrist Aquilino Polaino, amongst others), this is the basic fact that helps us to understand our times, the millennial cultural shift, a more important landmark than the journey to the moon or atomic energy. What is already called the 'dismantling of sexuality' (with contraception as a habit) opens the door to another phenomenon that is key to the course and fate of humanity: in vitro fertilization.

The results of this stage have lights and shadows. A sign of this is that since 1975 a certain tiredness has been perceived. Women were not as satisfied with the results of the second phase of feminism (which above all demanded sexual liberation) as they were with the first (the vote, education and economic independence). It was precisely in this year, at the World Conference of Women organized by the United Nations and also at later world conferences such as the one in 1995, that some feminist movements began to postulate and celebrate difference and complementariness more than radical equality. There is a certain revaluation of motherhood and the family. This is neo-feminism.

Elizabeth Badinter, for instance (although she shared de Beauvoir's posture on motherhood and abortion) claimed, 'To be similar to men, women have had to deny their feminine essence and become a pale copy of their masters. Losing their identity, they live the worst of alienation and unwittingly give the final victory to male imperialism.'[9]

Other famous feminists, too, began a revisionist stage. In her later years, Betty Friedan, the author of *The Feminine Mystique*[10] wrote another work, *The Fountain of Age*,[11] which denounced the feminist mystique as dogmatic and claimed women's right to transcend the traditional male model of success (professional and public) to rediscover the satisfactions of family intimacy.

Likewise, in 1984 Germaine Greer took on the Western anti-birth mentality so contrary to the wishes of women. Her book *Sex and Destiny*[12] had major repercussions along these lines. Women not only had to avoid being absorbed by mercantile society but they also had to attempt to get men to enter the private sphere. In short, and in the words of Jean Elshtain,[13] it was a question of putting an end to the modern trend to schematize the world by filling it with compartmentalization, such as, for example, that of the family versus work. Everybody, men and women alike, should be aware that the service and care carried out in the household domain also concerns men, unless they want to end up absorbed by two single preoccupations: power and competition.

Writers such as Virginia Held[14] defend the fact that relationships inside the home and those developed in motherhood can be a better model of social relationships than contracts or the market. Heir to a liberal individualism, civil society requires trust and, as a result, co-operation and solidarity. Here women can contribute a lot, as 'maternity has taught women not to separate their hearts from reason'.[15]

Finally, it is possible to talk of an anthropology that rediscovers the *richness of otherness*. There is no struggle between sexes or triumph based on identity between both sexes. Rather, there are two different, complementary ways of being a person: being a man and being a woman. Sex (despite what has constantly been claimed) is not solely cultural or biographical, although it is this, too. If we do not want to throw away everything achieved until now, if what we strive for is a new order between men and women and their respective roles in the world, we cannot ignore the specific nature of women: motherhood and their way of seeing the world and organizing life, which is complementary to that of men:

> In egalitarian feminism, the main engine of change was the legislator, who modified the laws and allowed equality with men by means of uniform legislation. In the feminism of difference, the central argument is motherhood, and it is necessary to protect women and to recognise their family and social contribution, and in this task legislators and politicians will also play an important role.[16]

Men and women: personal complementariness

Since the end of the 19th century and above all in the 20th, philosophy and psychiatry (Feuerbach, Freud, Jung) understood the importance of sex when comprehending human beings. Personalities are nothing without the sexual difference. There is no neutral person, so humans are by constitution male or female. However, excessive polarization in their physical aspects pollutes and spoils healthy relationships between men and women, spreading their influence to the rest of society. Human beings are personal beings, whose fundamental characteristic is rationality and the ownership of their decisions: freedom. At the same time, they need to love and to be loved. There is no 'I' without 'you'. 'A single person would be absolute misfortune',[17] because people are capable of giving themselves and this gift requires a recipient. Love does not exist without response. Human beings' rationality, sexuality and capacity to love allow them to be 'home builders'.[18]

Men and women as people are equal in the order of being. From the genetic standpoint, the difference between men and women is only 3 per cent, a small percentage, but one which is present in all the cells in our body. The consequence is clear: we are more equal than different, and at the same time, we are equal and different in everything. Being a man or being a woman entails a different way of seeing, understanding, evaluating and therefore acting in the world. In short, our biology also marks clear differences in male and female psychology, which are the basis of complementariness.

Only if there is clearly equality in difference will we be capable of seeing the world with a true global vision, that of both men and women, and therefore of redefining family roles, the distribution of household chores, the design of the working world and the acceptance of the social changes that this involves, as well as a new interpretation of history, of art, of psychology and of the other human sciences in light of this difference. Paradoxically, only in this way can we break down 'male' discriminations rooted far too long in our ways of doing and thinking.

There is, as is well known, proof that the hemispheres of the human brain are specialized: they speak different verbal and visual-spatial languages. Two types of thinking are even distinguished: the *male* (analytical, rational and quantitative) and the *female* (synthetic, intuitive and qualitative).

Men seem to have greater specialization in their cerebral hemispheres, so they can only communicate with each other formally, after coding the abstract representations. However, this does not happen in women; rather both hemispheres are capable of communicating less formally, in a less structured fashion and faster. *Time* magazine published some photographs illustrating this. It seems that when they think of a specific subject, men use one part of their brain, which appears with greater neuronal interconnections; women, however, present a complex neuronal lattice in action that occupies both hemispheres.

This explains why women are generally better than men at integrating verbal information with non-verbal, in assimilating all kinds of peripheral information rapidly. Maybe this is the root of the so-called *female intuition*, this ability to make a fast judgement that usually turns out right with respect to something or someone with whom they have only been for ten minutes.

Above all it must be made clear that virtues, or positive habits, are neither male nor female; they are personal. Each human being conquers them and develops them. However, philosophers and psychologists have insisted on highlighting 'the greater capacity to' or 'the inclination to' certain values of complementariness. Thus, when talking of the man–woman binomial, some authors[19] counterpoise certain terms: accurateness–analogy, superficial–deep, analysis–synthesis, discourse–intuition, competition–co-operation, growth–conservation, productive–reproductive.

From a more spatial point of view, men are identified with the line and the cube (human constructions) and women with the circle and the sphere, more in harmony with nature. From the standpoint of attitudes, long-term projects are talked of as opposed to the capacity to resolve with the minimal; magnanimity as opposed to the habit of economizing, bearing in mind present needs; inventing as opposed to maintaining; abstraction as opposed to specification; searching for rules as opposed to a greater tendency towards flexibility; prioritizing justice as opposed to a preference for mercy; quantitative measurement as opposed to qualitative evaluation; specialization as opposed to a holistic view.

However, despite the tendency of human intelligence towards these antagonisms, complete human beings require all of them, which is an invitation to learning, to exchange and to mutual enrichment.

From bestsellers[20] to press articles on the Internet,[21] there is agreement that women are naturally oriented towards interpersonal relations and tend to be interdependent, and that this is the basis of their security. While men are competitive and concentrate on achieving objectives and targets, women are co-operative and, without losing sight of the targets, they value the process leading up to achieving them.

When they sense hostility, men, being oriented towards action, physically release, and when something concerns them, they feel better actively resolving their problem. Women, on the other hand, are verbal and will release their hostility through words; in the same way, when they feel that their problems are being listened to, this contributes to their release. Words for us are not limited to transmitting information, they express feelings and thoughts and create ties of intimacy. When men feel under pressure or are distracted with other activities, 'they retreat to their caves' to resolve their problem. Women are disconcerted at this reaction; they prefer to talk everything over but must be capable of respecting men and patiently awaiting the outcome. Men will always end up 'leaving their cave', but always in their own time. A further example of the difference is each person's expectations with respect to relationships: women's primary need is to feel loved, be understood and listened to; that of men is to feel needed, which is why they are considered 'the providers' for the family. This is why job loss, for example, can cause men a terrible internal rupture, the same rupture that a woman would feel on losing a close personal relationship.

The family today

To complete this brief historical summary, we must remember that the family has passed through different chronological and historical stages. From an initial patriarchal model, in which the importance of the clan in some way determined the social and economic structure of society, we later moved on to a nuclear model made up of parents and children.

Today, couples generally prevail and there is a parallel fall in birth rates and increase in childless couples and marriages, in addition to single parent families. Within the family, the relationship between the mother and the father is no longer characterized by the traditional roles (she deals with the care-giving and he deals with the means of subsistence). In this new reality, families are more a unit of consumption or a mercantile company. And when children disappear as one of the primordial purposes of families, the natural consequence of the family unit, the social good that had to be protected, also disappears: the minor.

As mentioned in the introduction, the fact that women have now massively entered the job market does not mean that they all must do so or wish to do so. It is therefore a question of generating degrees of flexibility in the social structures so that they can adapt to the family and its needs at all times, and not the other way round. Chronologically, we might distinguish four models of family organization:

- M1: This is the most primitive and still holds in certain areas of the planet. Women work inside and outside home. This is the model of rural society.
- M2: This is the traditional division of roles. He works outside the home and she deals with looking after it. This was most frequent in the Spanish middle classes in the first two-thirds of the 20th century.
- M3: Both go out to work and she does a 'double shift'; that is, she also takes on the responsibilities at home.
- M4: Both work outside the home and share the household chores and child-rearing responsibilities. This is the model that some governments currently seem to want to promote.

But it should be said that there is also a fifth model, M5, which we should attain, in which each family opts for different alternatives at different times of its life cycle according to its needs, profile and preferences. It is therefore a question of enhancing the framework of the freedom of choice:

> I am a great enemy of single solutions. I believe that the important thing is that each person should have clear priorities and should freely choose and opt accordingly. The important thing is the priorities, which each family will reach through different means.
>
> (businesswoman, mother of three)

Legislation and some measures taken seem to be more focused on encouraging women to go out into the job market than on increasing true support for the family, which would enable free choice between remaining at home or combining home care with external work.

Table 1.1 summarizes the characteristics of three historical stages concerning the organization of work, remuneration, the relationship between the sexes and the balance between work and family. It can be seen that the frontiers between the two areas, work and family, are becoming more and more diffuse. There is an apparent conflict between roles: do men lose their masculinity because they share the working world with women? Is she any less feminine if she is not exclusively responsible for the child-rearing and internal organization of a home? The reply, above all in the 1960s, was summarized in

Table 1.1 Characteristics of three historical stages concerning the organization of work

	Work organization	Work remuneration	Implications of work remuneration	Relations between sexes	Work–family balance
Historically (before the Industrial Revolution)	Independent or interconnected units that exchange goods/ services	For yield in business units (one's own farm, workshop or shop)	The family itself distributes its time and both spouses balance their workload	Subordination of the female sex to the male; a sexist or chauvinistic model	Family and professional life are an undifferentiated unit.
Transition (1) (from the Industrial Revolution to the second half of the twentieth century)	Interdependent units with a growing number of connections among them, which begin to use value chains	Productivity in any of its manifestations is rewarded. As there is little dependency between some tasks and others, what is truly important is the individual contributions	• Productivity is measured by hours of service and availability • It is assumed that the ultimate responsibility of the husbands is to bring money into the home, and therefore the more they **work**, the more they fulfil their duty.	Subordination of the female sex to the male; a sexist or chauvinist model. At the end of this stage *formal equality* is achieved before the law.	Women are generally those who take on the housework whereas men have just one job outside the home and are paid

Current situation (2)	Dependent units: networks of value chains	*Theoretical:* • empowerment • teamwork (as it is assumed that the important thing in the new organization is interaction and the synergies of team work) *Real:* Individual contributions are still rewarded.	• Although the theoretical benefits of team work are known, individual success is rewarded • Time spent on and available for work is still seen as a measure of commitment to the company	The stage begins with theoretical equality before the law and evolves towards assimilationist models; male models are imposed on women. We are evolving towards true equal opportunities: fairness.	Women gradually enter the workplace; a new family and work model appears for men and women

(1) It is difficult to put dates on the years of transition between one situation and the other, as the borderline is diffuse and depends on the economic and social situation in each country.

(2) 'Current situation' is applicable to developed countries where women have already entered the working world in large numbers.

Source: Chinchilla, Las Heras, DPON-2, *Work as the Builder of the Individual, Family and Society: Looking at the Past and Projecting the Future,* IESE, 2002.

one phrase: 'We are equal, there are no roles!' Now, the new generations, the children of the previous ones, see things in a different way.
They ask for sufficient guarantees for there to be diversity, and they
want fairness (that each should be given what is appropriate) above
an equality resembling egalitarianism (giving the same to everyone
without bearing in mind special circumstances or specific moments).

Furthermore, we must remember that just as people have rights,
families do too, and this private domain must also include the right
to privacy. Although companies take measures, as we will see later,
and the state rolls out laws and policies in this respect, the specific
information on the employee and his or her family must be
respected without falling into the exhibitionism that is so often suffered by our society in the sensationalist press or the press also
known in Spanish as being 'of the heart'.

Women, work and family: a triangle in constant evolution

In the workplace, the consequence of women taking on men's roles
is *the penalization of motherhood*.[22]

In Spain, there is clear discrimination in company personnel hiring
not due to sex, but due to whether a women is or might be a mother.
In 86 per cent of cases involving candidates with the same aptitudes,
those hiring prefer young men. However, when the post requires
maturity and an older person, having been a mother starts to act as a
point in favour. In this sense, it would be possible to talk of the right
to be different as women's right to participate in public and working
life bearing in mind their maternity. The politician and writer, Janne
H. Matlary, proposes that 'this difference should be the basis of a
new restructuring of working conditions'.[23] This stance is not one of
inequality but true awareness of diversity. In fact, unequal treatment
in the end favours the whole group, but this change would be of
little use if men did not discover and fully exercise their fatherhood
as a complement to women's motherhood.

It is true that their close relationship with children might occasionally or temporarily reduce women's professional involvement, but in
any case it enriches their interpersonal and emotional life; it might
be a handicap when attempting to conquer hierarchical positions,
but it allows for a particularly intense dimension of feeling. Indeed,
if the pre-eminent place of women in family roles is sustained, it is

not only due to cultural pressure and potentially irresponsible male attitudes, but also to the dimensions of feelings, of power and of autonomy that accompany women's maternal functions.

Maternity involves a special communion with the mystery of life that matures in women. Women's unique contact with the new being that is forming also creates an attitude towards humankind, not only towards the children themselves but towards people in general, that profoundly characterizes their entire personality. In fact, women engender and carry another being within themselves, allowing them to grow inside, offering them the necessary space and respecting them in all their otherness. Therefore, women perceive and teach that human relationships are true if they are open to welcoming another person, recognized and loved for the dignity they have as a person and not other factors, such as usefulness, strength, intelligence, beauty or health.

By relinquishing being a mother, women have become more available to ensure their position in the working world. However, now women are not sure that this is the best way to remain there. Cases are cited of women who postpone having their first child by five or six years, and when they become pregnant they are dismissed due to 'low performance, lack of interest in the company or little commitment'. This practice continues *de facto* despite the new law reconciling family and working life, which considers such dismissal improper. The difficult conditions if this employee is readmitted to the company lead to their being encouraged to leave the company in exchange for compensation. It is also true that there are other companies, in contrast, which are beginning to view one's personal and family life as important and worthy of policies that make it reconcilable with work, and which might be a source of competence and equilibrium for employees:

> We decided to have a child and it cost me my job. I didn't like that company, its style, the route to promotion was not clear, and women were systematically dismissed when they became pregnant and I knew it. I took them to court, I was readmitted, but I never started again because the company did not want me to. But I won my case, and this is what is important. I have never talked about this for fear of being labelled conflictive, but this is part of my history.
>
> (consultant, 40, one daughter)

In the United States, 49 per cent of women executives do not have children, compared to 19 per cent of men at the same level. The reason is quite simple: in most cases they are generally not even married. Whereas 83 per cent of male senior executives are married, women are only married 50 per cent of the time.

As regards remaining on the market, the figures speak for themselves. In addition to the great differences between men and women in terms of their participation in the job market and unemployment, the 1998 data from the Economic and Social Council indicate that Spanish people from 20 to 44 years of age without children have an employment rate of 67 per cent. Spaniards of the same age with children under five have an employment rate of 40 per cent, the lowest in the European Union and almost 20 points below the average. The evidence is clear: for many women, family responsibilities entail a withdrawal from the job market. Spain must reach a balance and seek the most appropriate route, bearing in mind that in Spain resources set aside for family aid are between four and seven times below the European average.

Maybe this view of motherhood as a handicap influences women's attitude in the working world, something that is reflected in the writings of the feminist author Christian Collange,[24] now a family specialist, and the sociologist Lipovetsky[25] as well as in several sociological studies, such as the one commissioned by Harvard University to Betty Friedan in 1983. The best and brightest entered this prestigious academic institution, yet a high percentage of women did not manage to develop their full potential and never fully stood out. One of Friedan's hypotheses is that they adopted the role of men to better adapt to a male structure and style. They were frightened of being themselves. As one of the deans of the institution said, 'We get the most brilliant women of course. Their academic records are impressive as are the results of their admission tests. However for some reason, when they are here they do not seem to fare well. How can this be explained?'[26] It seems that we are faced with yet one more case that brings forth the strategy of assimilation. Maybe this situation is the main reason why some currents of modern-day feminism have rediscovered femininity and motherhood precisely as points for making affirmative claims. True female ambition assumes having the social and working conditions necessary for developing as women in all potential aspects of their femininity.

In the face of this reality, the model of equal opportunity emerged with strength in the 1980s, understood as *equality in difference*. Women, they say, should not only *appear in*, but should also intervene in making the laws about them and the situation derived from their motherhood. From the famous cry 'my body is mine', we should now shift to a cry of 'my child is mine.'

Contemporary authors such as Giddens say that the subject of the family, and therefore that of motherhood, has been framed in a new political and social thought called the *culture of separation* or dualistic culture, which works by separating and dividing the realities that are interrelated in life, such as soul and body, human being and nature, I and the other, woman and man, family and work, sexuality and procreation, work and motherhood.

In this sense, it is interesting to highlight the contribution of the *Communitarian Manifesto* signed in 1992 by Mary Ann Glendon, Etzioni and fifty other intellectuals specialized in the field, stating the need for both partners, mother and father, in proper child-rearing. This is the so-called 'family-oriented' culture, the aim of which is integration – the marriage of peers, the marriage of equals – as opposed to the culture of separation.

Only from complementariness, equality in difference, can men and women say, 'Let's make the world, culture, company and family together.' Only from this viewpoint will each be able to contribute specific ways of being and acting for mutual enrichment, without one ridiculously attempting to assimilate to the other's way of being. Just as children need the love and attention from both the father and mother, the working world and social life are awaiting the female 'genius' to make them more habitable, so that they adapt to personal needs in each stage of life, so that each person in each circumstance might give the best of themselves. In turn, the working world demands the presence of the woman-mother to depend on the person and the family, and not the other way round:

To be a woman and a mother should be like a sterile capsule, isolated, which others must respect. External effects must not affect this reality. Anyone who understands this will achieve what they want in life. *We must protect motherhood.* Today, preserving the family and everything this involves is more difficult; freedom and economic independence and geographic mobility oblige each of the members of the couple to struggle much more. It is necessary to safeguard time for the family, knowing when and at what time they are the priority.

(businesswoman, 70, three children and five grandchildren)

International public bodies, such as the United Nations, have on different occasions reminded us that without the family we are heading for chaos. Article 30 of the Platform for Action or the Beijing declaration (1995) recognizes that 'women make a great contribution to the well-being of families and the development of society, the importance of which is not yet recognized or given due consideration'; and it continues:

it is necessary to recognise the social importance of motherhood and the function of both parents in the family and the upbringing of the children, which requires both (women and men) and society as a whole to share responsibility. Motherhood, being a parent and women's role in procreation should not be a reason for discrimination nor should it restrict women's full participation in society. It is also necessary to recognise the important role women play in many countries in caring for other members of family.

Women who abandon their femininity and admire men to the extent of imitating them end up swallowed by the system and may not be positive agents of change. At the beginning they might triumph externally because their adaptation to the masculine world is complete, but sooner or later frustration will come: 'Who am I? What have I positively contributed to the world I live in?'

Even for reasons of common sense it is necessary to consider how wrong it is to imitate men. In the long run, focusing life, organizing work, resolving problems like men is more wasteful and brings few results simply because they are men and we are not. Only by highlighting diversity do we mutually enrich ourselves and as a result will be able to respect each other.

On the other hand, viewing this matter as merely role distribution means turning it into a dialectic struggle, and this would be a mistake. Neither sex is waging a battle to displace the other in the family, in work, in culture or in society. It is a question of adding, sharing and perfecting life, which, in the end, belongs to both, always with the idea of freedom, but a responsible freedom that seeks co-operation and is based on respect. As the Austrian psychiatrist Victor Frankl said, 'Next to the Statue of Liberty a monument should be erected in homage to responsibility',[27] and he is certainly not mistaken.

In addition to being a man or woman, each individual has a biography, goals and aptitudes. No institutional power can mark the sign of this silent revolution, they should only have sufficient sensitivity to know what is happening and engender a social and legal framework that facilitates new forms of work and social organization that view the family as an essential core that must be protected in society, but one that is, at the same time, dynamic and participatory. It is therefore not acceptable to talk about a female social space, for women can and must be in all spheres of family, work and politics. Women are those who must define what feminism means today by their actions, giving signs of their will, their desire, their true ambition.

The way is gradually being paved for a new *integrative feminism*. This is the feminism of complementariness, of co-operation with men in all areas of life (family, culture, company and society) which requires a critical mass of women capable and suitable for it in key positions, basically in decision-making bodies (legislative, labour, political, entrepreneurial) and a special sensitivity from men to understand this reality and support the changes. Two key ideas therefore close this chapter: women are already in the working world and are not going anywhere, and the family belongs to both men and women, fathers and mothers. In the words of the anthropologist Blanca Castilla, the challenge is as ambitious as 'creating a society with a mother and a family with a father'.[28] On a hopeful note, what some already call family fever is also infecting fathers. According to a survey made by Radcliffe Public Policy Centre, more than 80 per cent of men between 21 and 39 years of age would like to have a job open to children. Maybe soon we will hear more often:

> I have decided that my children should truly come into my life and get in the way. I recognize that I have not got very good marks as a father and husband recently. If it is of any use, I have turned down a job where things could have been worse in this sense.
>
> (marketing manager, 37, two children)

In the United States some have already 'dropped out'. Danny O'Neill resigned as the managing director of Britannic to become a part-time consultant for the company. The reason was that he preferred to have more time to play football with his nine-year-old triplets. At first nobody praised him; now he's a national hero.

However, although it is important to take decisions on a personal level, it will often be difficult to take them if they are not backed by public policies in support of the family, and this is precisely what we will deal with in the following chapter.

2

The Family: Current Situation and Legal Framework

'The family is the natural, fundamental element of society.'
Declaration of Human Rights, Art. 16.3

'The main priority in family policy is to establish measures that enable family and professional life to be reconciled.'
European Union Charter of Fundamental Rights

After the Industrial Revolution, the economic and social structure underwent significant change. First, a new company model appeared that was more productive and competitive; at the same time, society was built around individuals viewed as voters (in the political domain) and producers (in the economic domain). Society was no longer based on the family unit and became subservient to the rights of the individual. Since then, the 'official' strength of the family in society has diminished in favour of other groups or civil, economic or cultural entities.

Despite everything, in the individual domain, the family has continued to exist strongly and solidly as an irreplaceable unit for people, even though in the past three decades it has suffered attacks based on the pre-eminence of independence, freedom and self-realization as opposed to stable bonds.

In a family, each member is loved for what they are and not for what they have or achieve. Additionally, with love as a family's reason for being and destiny, it is the best school of values for life and also of personal and professional competencies for the workplace. Only when the family does not emerge with a permanent mission does fear appear in all of its varieties: the fear of others, of failing or being failed, the fear of having children, the fear of educating in a certain way, etc.

Therefore, both the company and the state must change the course of their economic reasoning. Instead of *thinking in the short term* – what the family costs in terms of direct and indirect aid, in family-responsible policies and new ways of hiring – they should *think in the long term* – what the non-family costs in the light of the reversal of the population pyramid with a considerable fall in the working population.

The non-family, in addition to being anti-economic, causes an educational vacuum that gives rise to higher crime rates and more psychological problems in society, which then have to be dealt with by the state through its social spending. Without social capital generated mainly in the family, there is no true wealth. This is how Francis Fukuyama, author of *The Great Disruption*, sees it.[1] For this thinker, the onslaught of individualism has grown at the same time as a society based on formal rules or laws as opposed to the family as the centre of co-existence with informal, but firm laws. Planned order appears to supersede spontaneous order, and the state is obliged to legislate even the smallest details. The technological revolution that has enabled the massive, full entry of women into the working world has not, and this is the paradox, enabled them to devote more time to children, to their upbringing, and so people grow up with a mistrust of institutions and difficulty co-operating with others. It is as if the social capital in advanced society were shrinking. Perhaps we forget that the family is the first setting of education and society and the basis of all others. As the psychiatrist Enrique Rojas says, 'Education is the structure of the individual edifice; culture is merely the decoration.'[2]

Nowadays, everyone wants to support the family, but in order to continue to fulfil its mission without having to oblige parents to perform a thousand heroic acts each day, the family needs better political, economic and social conditions. Today more than ever, enterprise, family and society are a triangle in constant evolution at the centre of which is the person who is formed or deformed through these three areas. For the family to continue to be a space of personal development and humanization for its members, work needs to be redefined to allow it to be so.

In the last fifty years, the tendency has been to increasingly view a profession as a sign of personal identity in such a way that it has become an absolute, a priority, an excluding value. Some go as far as to say that if we do not work we are not citizens. The case of women is even more extreme: household work is relegated to second place and if women do not work outside the home, they will not be capable of showing society their worth. This is all the result of a myopic view of the household situation which is granted no value because it is unpaid. As Machado said, 'All idiots confuse value with price.'

The concept of personal success is also affected by this view. The growing encroachment of consumer society has suffocated other areas which express and realize the human spirit, but which are unpaid. This is the case with housework, the irreplaceable support to families by grandparents, as well as affectively integrating role of caring for the sick, and all altruistic activities we perform for the benefit of others.

New times: things have changed

Our society is full of paradoxes. A few years ago the debate focused on the protection of life after birth and not before; we were immersed in the pros and cons of abortion. Many were convinced that what the maternal womb shelters does not exist, and the law decided to protect the being only when it could walk in the street or sleep in a cot. Now, with a shortage of children, we are beginning to defend not only the unborn, recovering the wisdom of Roman law by which the foetus was subject to law, but even the imagined child, the child that does not even exist and which politicians of all colours are suddenly willing to defend.

The INE's 1999 fertility survey reveals that 36.42 per cent of Spanish families have still not had the number of children they would like to have. The reasons given for this are: a shortage of economic resources (30.82 per cent),[3] health problems (17.08 per cent) and a wish or the need to work outside the home (14.06 per cent).[4] In addition, the birth rates are falling drastically, from 2.8 children per woman in 1975 to 1.2 in the year 2002 according to the CIS. Today, Spain is in last place in the European Union in terms of generational replacement, thus jeopardizing its pension system. The phenomenon of immigration has in part corrected this imbalance; in Catalonia for example, in the year 2000, half of the children born were born to immigrants.

Only when the European Union forces us to reach higher employ-ment levels to approach European convergence levels (7.8 per cent is the average) and thus palliate our unemployment rate (at 12.9 per cent, the highest in the Euro zone)[5] do we reconsider things. Furthermore, most women believe that the period established by current legislation for caring for children is clearly insufficient in comparison with other European countries. For example, Finland, a pioneering country in women's public participation in political life, provides excellent maternity conditions: 68 per cent of women take the 11-month maternity leave stipulated by law, and during this time they receive up to 75 per cent of their salary. In France, the April 2003 reform has been called the 'wage for becoming a mother'. It is a bonus of €800 that pregnant women receive shortly before giving birth, an amount which adds to the €160 a month received as of the fifth month of pregnancy and the supplements and allowances for parents who decide to give up work to look after their children.

In any case, today Europe is a paradoxical continent. According to data from the European Observatory on the social situation of the family, countries with traditional demographic growth in the 1960s and 1970s saw their rates fall below the replacement level. In 1975, when Spain had one of the highest birth rates, with 2.8 children per woman, almost all European Union countries had already reached very low rates. Today, only Macau, Bulgaria and Latvia have lower rates than Spain. According to the United Nations, since 1995 Spanish women have had 1.1 children, whereas the world average is 2.6 children per woman and the European average is 1.5. This is aggra-vated by the gradual advancement of the average age for giving birth (30.5 years in Spain as opposed to 27 in Austria), which places us alongside Holland as the front-runners in delaying women's first birth. Furthermore, the average age of young people still living with their parents has increased (90 per cent of those between 20 and 24 years of age and 60 per cent of those between 25 and 29). In the majority of cases, what explains this tendency is the delay in reaching the economic independence required for being able to form a family or simply to live away from home.

According to data published by the INE in 1999, childless couples have increased by 9.5 per cent compared to 1990, and couples with two children have fallen by 12.2 per cent. Between 1990 and 1997, marital separations increased by 50 per cent, divorces by 47 per cent and the average age for marrying rose to 30 for men and 28 for women. In Spain in 42 per cent of childless couples both members work, 44 per cent for couples with children. It has been calculated that the number of couples with double incomes has increased by 12 per cent in eight years.[6]

In the past three decades, we have been witness to what has undoubtedly been one of the most important socio-demographic changes in the post-industrial working world. For the first time, women have entered the job market *en masse*: 191 million in the European Union, in other words, 51.2 per cent of the population. In the year 2000, the percentage of participation according to Eurostat ranged from 40.3 per cent in Spain to 72.1 per cent in Denmark. Only 6.3 per cent of employed men work part-time compared to 33.7 per cent of women. In absolute numbers, 18 per cent of the working population of the European Union works in part-time jobs.

In Holland, a country where 40 per cent of contracts are part-time, work teams are semi-virtual and physical presence in the office is only sporadic. On the other hand, it is necessary to highlight that in Europe, above all in the more developed in northern countries, female unemployment has not risen any more and seems to have reached the ceiling, and has even fallen in some cases. This trend confirms the study we mentioned in the first chapter: 20 per cent of women put work before the family, 60 per cent reconcile both things or want to do so and the final 20 per cent prefer to remain at home to look after their families.

According to the 2000 Eurobarometer, for 97 per cent of Spanish women the family is an essential value; however, public policies designed to support it are advancing very tentatively. In our country, the percentage social spending on the family with respect to the national budget, according to data from Eurostat 2002, is 2.1 per cent of the GDP, whereas the European Union average is 8.5. We still do not have a state agreement that harmonizes and unifies family aid in the different Spanish autonomous regions. Having a Ministry of the Family would ensure a cross-wise approach to this basic institution of society. In this way, any decision (tax, transport, work, etc.) taken by the government would have someone responsible for gauging its impact. It is a question of urgent measures to support the family ceasing to be considered mere 'subsidies', thus making the family institution a social reality with full legal rights.

The legal framework: aid, state policies and legislation

The state is responsible for arbitrating measures to ensure citizens' growth, training and well-being. Therefore, in this section we will focus on the different policies developed in the European states in support of the family and the results achieved. The initiatives taken from political bodies are of the utmost importance as they determine the context in which the development of this basic institution is fostered or encumbered in our society. The laws are also the frame of reference for all society, including companies.

As Professor Lecaillon of the University of Paris II Pantheon-Assas rightly sums up, 'today it is a real challenge to have a family'; mothers and fathers are true 'entrepreneurs': they decide to have children and raise them, bringing wealth into society often without much support. Moreover, Professor Shirley Burgaff suggests that

> modern society should establish a social contract for the family of the same size as the family's contribution to the economic system . . . a small revolution would consist of the pension system becoming parenthood dividends. For example, obliging children to pay the taxes that make up the national pension system so that they might then become pension plans for their parents.[7]

It is fair to recognize their contribution and make a call to everyone for responsibility in order to prevent the source from drying up. Europe today lacks a common concept of what the family is; the family is the competence of each state and there is little concordance among different state policies. Only with a change of perspective along these lines will it be possible to talk of a new 'sustainable development' applied to people. It is not enough to nurture birth policies; support must be given to the upbringing of these children in all stages. Only in this way will each country have a healthy population of citizens capable of becoming productive in all senses (economic, social . . .). 'All family policies must be considered long-term investments with clear returns, and never merely subsidies or supports. Having a general European framework on family policy would be the ideal start. The family as a basic cell of society must be immersed in communities of stable people with institutional recognition on all levels in order to be able to develop'.[8]

Do public policies foster conciliation of family and working life? Do they support families in which both parents work outside the home? Although we have referred at different times to two indicators, fertility and female employment, the aim of these policies should not be to directly and exclusively ensure that these increase, but rather to guarantee a framework of freedom that enables each family to design their way of life depending on their capacities, needs and expectations and the needs of their offspring.

Article 16 of the European Council's Revised Social Charter specifies the states' responsibility:

> In order to make the living conditions essential for the full development of the family, the basic unit of society, the signatories agree to promote the economic, legal and social protection of the life of the family, particularly through social and family allowances, tax regulations, incentives for the construction of housing adapted to the needs of families, aid for new homes and all other suitable measures.

In June 2001, at the twenty-seventh session of the Conference of European Ministers entrusted with family matters, the different policies and mechanisms in the Council of Europe member states were examined with reference to workers with family responsibilities. From the comparative study of the reports submitted by the member states, one can glean that their national policies and mechanisms have the following main objectives:

To make working timetables more flexible;
To help families with young children;
To help families with persons dependent due to physical or mental incapacity, age or early childhood needs;
To equally share family responsibilities between the man and the woman.

Along the same lines, a group of experts from the Council of Europe is currently developing programmes intended to enhance equality between men and women in the working world. In October 2001, promoting equality was enshrined as a guiding principle for implementing all employment programmes on a local level. Based on this principle, women, particularly those who have family responsibilities, are entitled to benefit from training or aid programmes that correspond to their situation, such as, for example, day nurseries that provide quality services at a reasonable price. In addition to this, flexible working timetables are being promoted (part-time work, telecommuting, etc.), which should be offered under equal conditions to all working men or women with family responsibilities. Having reached this point, we can talk about four levels of initiatives.

Legislation on motherhood/fatherhood and specific conciliation measures

Maternity leave is a general policy throughout Europe that allows pregnant women to take a break from their professional activity to be able to deal with care before and after birth. Its duration and characteristics vary from one country to another. Community directive 92/85 establishes a minimum 14 weeks, which holds in such various countries as Germany, Ireland, Portugal and even Sweden. In Spain, the duration is 16 weeks, a period longer than that stipulated by the European directive although shorter than the 24 weeks in Denmark, the 22 weeks in Italy or the 11 months in Finland. In Spain it is possible to take a maximum of 10 weeks before the birth, although there is an obligation to take at least six weeks after the birth.

In some countries, women are able to receive full pay for the whole of the period or for part of it; in other countries, this payment may be a percentage of their salary. The maternity leave may be compulsory or optional in the sense that, in some countries, only part of the maternity leave is compulsory.[9] Mothers are thus allowed to choose between a shorter time period which is fully paid or a longer period with lower pay.[10]

Working women with family responsibilities receive aid in many countries (working leaves, etc.), *because it is understood that they are the ones who have to deal with the household*. In other words, it is believed that the childcare duties are the exclusive realm of the women, which is simply fallacious, because the children of working parents need to see both their mother and their father.[11]

Therefore, in legislation, an attempt is being made to establish identical rules for the father and the mother so that they might both benefit from child-rearing leave to deal with their children during their childhood.[12] In fact, in some countries such as Denmark,[13] the public authorities include this field in a general programme to promote equality between the sexes and, as has already been said, economic measures are being extended, particularly paternity leave, to allow both parents to truly participate in bringing up their children.[14] There are even countries that sanction the non-use of paternity leave with the understanding that this jeopardizes the interests of the mother.[15]

Paternity leave is a specific, non-transferable right for fathers, aside from the possibility of joint use of parental leave. Sweden is a pioneer in this field, granting 10 days with partial payment after birth and an additional 30 days (not transferable to the woman). In Spain, paternity leave only lasts two days, which may be extended by a further two days if travel is required, and this is fully paid. There are very similar conditions in Belgium, Germany, France, Luxembourg, Holland and Portugal, although in the latter two countries this leave is not payable by law. In Denmark, fathers are entitled to two weeks' leave in the fourteen following birth. In Finland, this is three weeks and four in Norway. In the latter country, fathers may also benefit from other allowances or subsidies and these four weeks are exclusive for men; otherwise the leave time is deducted from the almost one year shared by both spouses. The result is that almost 80 per cent of Norwegian men take this leave to look after their children. This is explained by Jens Stoltenberg, the Norwegian Prime Minister in 2000: 'It is possible to combine work and family if society offers a suitable framework and the government considers it a priority policy. The formula is simple: paternity leave, greater responsibility of men in domestic and family life, and aid from the state.'[16] A similar case can be seen with the Finnish prime minister Paavo Lipponen, who took paternity leave when his two daughters were born. 'In this way,' he said, 'a new masculinity is arising, a culture of fatherhood that is very positive for children.'[17]

Childcare leave: Leave to raise or care for children exists in quite a few European countries[18] and allows a worker, male or female, who is the parent of young children to take a break from their job in order to be with them in their early years. In some countries, the allowance is generous; in others less so.[19] Some countries also allow *adoption leave*.[20]

These leaves vary among countries: three paid months in Belgium; the same amount of time in Greece and Ireland but unpaid: six months in Italy and Luxembourg; a part-time leave in Holland and Finland; and fourteen months in Sweden. The time in which this period may be taken is also different: until the child is three in Germany, Spain,[21] France and Portugal; and until the child is at most eight in Denmark, Holland and Sweden.

Direct aid for the family and more specifically economic subsidies depending on the number of children, starting from the second and third child, regardless of income level

Today there are *family subsidies* in a large number of European countries, following a variety of formulae: subsidies for birth, family, education, health, maternity pay, aid for families who adopt or act as foster families, those with the economic difficulties or the socially excluded, housing, allowances to pay for nurseries or school transport, allowances for the education of children of unemployed people. There are also insurance policies to maintain income levels during periods of unemployment.[22]

In Spain, following the decentralization of the state into autonomous communities, a large part of this aid has also been decentralized. According to the Institute of Family Policy in its third report presented in May 2003, 30 per cent of the autonomous communities still give no type of direct aid to families (Madrid, Extremadura, La Rioja, Balearic Islands and Asturias). This percentage rises to almost 50 per cent if we consider that Aragon, the Canary Islands and Valencia only give direct aid for a multiple births starting with triplets. Compared to 2002, more autonomous communities have given such aid: Galicia, Cantabria and Valencia. Others, such as Navarre, Castilla-La Mancha and Castilla-Leon have increased the types of allowances and three more (Catalonia, Basque Country and Castilla-Leon) have increased the amounts.

Going into detail, in Navarre it is possible to apply for €330 in direct aid per month starting from the second child, and this amount is received until the child is one year old. Furthermore, numerous families receive €360 in aid per year for each child under 18 starting from the fourth child. Catalonia provides across the board aid of €481 a year starting from the first child and lasting until the child is three years old. In the case of a large family, this amount rises to €600 and is extended to six years. In the Basque Country, the amount is even higher: €1,100 starting from the second child and lasting until the child is five. The government of Castilla-Leon, one of the autonomous communities with most serious problems of population ageing, shows family sensitivity by applying measures such as paying €1,803 for the birth of a third child, but as long as the annual income of the family unit is no more than €36,060.

Another advantage is that both working mothers and the company for which they work are exempt from paying social security during the first year of motherhood.

Indirect or tax aid for income tax, thus variable depending on income level

Companies have deductible expenses ... families sometimes do not appear to have them. Gérard François Dumont of the Institute of Political Demography of the University of Paris says:

> In the first place, to improve the current situation it is necessary to set up a policy that truly allows decisions to be freely taken. Young people must have the opportunity to start a family with favourable housing policies, and families must be able to choose the number of children they wish to have, which involves the need for tax and social policies that do not place them at a disadvantage. Even seeing things from an economic standpoint, children are human capital and therefore parents' spending on raising their children is an investment and must be tax deductible, just like company investments.

Experts agree that a good family policy cannot be based only on one kind of measure, whether direct (subsidies) or indirect (tax). As we shall see below, the different European states have combined direct and indirect measures on most occasions. Tax deductions are generally small and ridiculous, working more according to income levels than of the number of children, and in the end they act more as aid to alleviate social poverty.

As defended by Eugenio Simón Acosta, Professor of Financial and Tax Law at the University of Santiago de Compostela, one possible solution would be for income tax to be paid taking into account each individual's true capacity to pay, that is, based on the income available after deducting the costs of feeding and maintaining the family. We thus enter a new concept of income: family income.

Raising a child, that is maintenance plus education, costs between €4,800 and €10,200 a year (800,000 and 1,700,000 pesetas), and from the time a child is born until they are 18, between €108,000 and €180,000 (18 and 30 million pesetas). What does the Spanish state do? The new income tax establishes a monthly payment of €100 for each child under three for mothers who work outside the home. One measure seeks to foster two things at the same time: the birth rate and the entry of women into the working world. The monthly payment may be exchanged for a deduction of €1,200 from the income tax declaration. In any case, this is not a universal allowance, that is, for all mothers, or support for motherhood itself. It is only a type of aid for mothers working outside the home, although what would be truly equitable and fair would be for all mothers to receive this amount simply for being mothers. Then it would be the child that is 'rewarded' or 'helped', not the fact of working.

As regards other measures, the determining factor is income level. Parents whose income fails to exceed €7,950 a year may ask the social security for €291 a month in aid. This solution is, in fact, a social aid, in other words, a supplement for low incomes, not family aid.

To sum up, the deductions allowed in the new income tax system are as follows:

- €1,400 for the first child, €1,500 for the second, €2,200 for third and €2,300 for the fourth and following children. In other words, €1,400 for one child, €2,900 for two children, €5,100 for three children and €7,400 for four children, followed by an additional €2,300 for each further child.
- Starting from the first child, there are enormous differences among autonomous communities, from €36 per child in the Canary Islands to €1,502 in Navarre.
- A deduction of €1,200 for mothers for each child under three, this amount being added to the general deduction or being paid in the form of direct aid of €100 a month for working mothers.
- €800 for families with members over 65 years of age. An additional deduction has also been created for assisting relatives who live with people over 75 years of age.

State-enhanced infrastructures for the family

Nursery services fulfil a constantly increasing demand, and developing them is a priority in several European countries.[23] The aim is to offer both parents the chance to work and to guarantee them a free place for their children under school age in an institution or a subsidy earmarked to pay for nursery care. It seems clear that a well-organized system of nurseries is a necessary condition today to reconcile raising children with employment. Two measures put forward are direct aid: the nursery cheque (a measure that extends the capacity to choose to which nursery or school people wish to take their children without further loading the fixed structure of the public sector, a clear example of the principle of subsidiarity), and tax deductions for companies that provide nurseries as yet another service for their employees.

For companies, another deductible expense (specifically 10 per cent of corporate tax) is that of nursery expenses for the children of their employees, both those within the company and if the company decides to help directly by giving their employees money for such services.

In Spain, only 2 per cent of children under three years of age have a place in nurseries financed by the public sector, compared to 50 per cent in Germany, 48 per cent in Denmark, 33 per cent in Sweden and 31 per cent in Norway.[24] While in Denmark, Sweden, Belgium, France and Finland most children under three go to public nurseries, in other countries such as Spain, Ireland or the United Kingdom they are in a minority. Furthermore, as an interesting footnote, in more advanced countries such as Holland and Germany, 24-hour nurseries are beginning to open, where children with different disabilities may also receive care.

As regards the percentage of the elderly who receive care at home, in Spain they only account for 1 per cent as opposed to 24 per cent in Finland, 17 per cent in Denmark, 14 per cent in Norway and 13 per cent in Sweden and Switzerland.[25] In Spain, there are around 1,200,000 dependent people, the majority of whom are cared for at home by relatives. In figures, 90 per cent of women between the ages of 35 and 65 who stay at home each day do so because they have to look after a dependent person.[26]

Some developments towards flexibility in Europe

European states have developed different formulae to introduce greater flexibility in working timetables. Amongst others, these include:

- Reductions in the normal working day[27]
- Part-time work or timetable adjustments[28]
- Tele-commuting, or the possibility of working at home in such a way that one can combine professional and household work at the same time[29]
- The right to be absent from work due to family obligations[30]
- The temporary extension of the working day: for a period of three to six months a worker may extend their working day to up to 48 hours a week in order to have a reduction in their timetable in the following period[31]
- Time credits: workers may momentarily take a break from their professions in order to spend a certain period of time dealing with family or personal needs. This interruption may occur at any time and for as long as the worker might decide[32]
- Work formulae: workers may choose between different working timetables proposed by the employer.[33]

In Spain, although there have been great developments in legislation, timetable flexibility in its different permutations has often remained mere theory. There is the conviction that hours of presence are the same as productivity and that two people working four hours each do not produce as much as one working eight. However, reality has shown us that the greater the flexibility, the greater the versatility, creativity and productivity. A long path still remains for this to be accepted. Generally speaking, it is not usually the company that takes the first step towards this flexibility, and they usually react by defending themselves, saying, 'We have always done it this way', which is understandable for people who rely on their success in a context of hard competition. However, there are companies that manage to discover the many advantages to be had from adopting measures intended to enhance home–work conciliation. In other countries, this attitude is nurtured by awards for 'The most favourable company for women and families' or by awareness-raising campaigns on the subject of 'Family and Work'[34] or on the advantages of a balance between working and private life.[35] In Spain, civil society has also recently moved to help to raise businesses' awareness, and to this end the newspaper *Expansión*, Vodafone, Sanitas and IESE have worked along with CVA, the communications company, to make it possible to convene and present the 'Flexible Company Award: towards a balance between working and personal life.'

Likewise, in some countries there are examples of national agreements between the government and the different social stakeholders (unions, business organizations, farmers' associations, etc.),[36] with the aim of developing policies that favour the interests of the family. In the case of Spain, by signing a protocol with more than twenty companies and the +Family Foundation, the government is committed to starting up a pioneering certification in Europe: that of the Family-Responsible Company (FRC), backed by the Ministry of Work and Social Affairs.

Types of countries in terms of aid

In short, in the light of these brief notes, it is clear that family measures in Europe vary depending on the type of welfare state and the objectives pursued. For example, the policy in Scandinavian countries fulfils the dual objective of women being able to work outside the home and have children at the same time. That of France comes in response to the keenly felt need to increase the number of French people. However, the objective of increasing the birth rate does not seem of particular interest to governments in the United Kingdom and Germany. These two countries have also been affected by low birth rates, which jeopardize the financing of pension programmes and health spending, constantly on the increase, for an ageing population. Despite this, neither of these countries has explicitly adopted policies aimed at increasing the birth rate.

According to Martin Spielauer,[37] the Director of the Department of Socio-economic Research at the Austrian Institute of Family Studies, four types or models of family policies could be established according the existing combination or proportion of two variables: direct economic support and infrastructures (see Table 2.1).

The success of France is well known to all, where in recent years there has been greater support for families, birth rates and two-income families. Sweden, however, the welfare state par excellence, chose a

Table 2.1   Four models of family policies

	Economic support	
Infrastructure	Freedom of choice *France* Traditional *Germany*	Pro-egalitarian *Sweden* Non interventionist *United Kingdom*

model where the public sector took on the functions of the private sector, something very different from Germany, which is more traditional and in favour of direct economic support rather than service improvement. The United Kingdom is an example of a non-interventionist country in this sense. Although it is famous for its broad social policy, it seems that having children there is a private matter.

In short, there are two variables that communicate the success of policies: the birth rate and the female employment index. France has reached second place in the birth rate ranking in the European Union with more than 1.8 children per woman and a female employment rate of 52 per cent. This country provides a 16-week maternity leave at 85 per cent pay. The state also guarantees the person's job for two years and offers three years of financial benefits for families with more than one child. Nursery places are guaranteed for children starting from the age of two, there are no jumps in time or attendance vacuums that endanger the careers of mothers who also work.[38]

Germany has a clearly lower birth rate: 1.3 children per woman and an employment index of 55 per cent. In this country, after 14 weeks of maternity leave paid at 100 per cent there is a payment of €307 for 24 months or €460 for 12 months. However, the problem is the insufficient nursery network, particularly for children under three; schools also finish at midday. As a result, Germany has a high percentage of women who have no children.

Sweden has a birth rate of 1.5 children per woman and one of the highest female employment rates in the European Union, almost equal to that of men (68 per cent for women and 70 per cent for men). The infrastructures are also in the vanguard and are supplemented with one year's leave at 90 per cent pay, three months of financial benefits and guaranteed childcare covered by the state once the child is one year old.

Table 2.2 The current situation in Spain

Autonomous Community	Does it offer direct aid?	Type of aid	Amount (euros)	Income limits (euros)	Children	Age limit (length of allowance)	Other conditions
Castilla-Leon	Yes	Aid for birth or adoption: First child	Universal 601.01	For incomes under 21,035.42		Single payment	
		Second child Third child First child	1,202.02 1,803.04 301.01	For incomes over 21,035.42			
		Second child Third child Aid for requesting leave to look after children	301.01 901.04 The amount will be 100% for workers with a minimum inter-professional salary of 708	Family income may not exceed 36,060.73	The leave may not be less than one year		
		Aid for adoption	50% increase		For the first two children		

Table 2.2 (Continued)

Autonomous Community	Does it offer direct aid?	Type of aid	Amount (euros)	Income limits (euros)	Children	Age limit (length of allowance)	Other conditions
		Aid for multiple births or adoptions	100% increase		For the third and successive children		For expenses associated with certification of appropriateness
Aragon	No	Multiple births	Undefined. Maximum 1,200	Income limit 8,400	From triplets	Up to 6	After evaluating the application
Canary Islands	Yes	Multiple births	Variable according to number born and parents' income. Maximum amount of 1,202.02 per child per year	Per capita income under 8,414.16 per year	Triplets or more	Budgetary allocation 2003: 18,030	
Catalonia	Yes	Aid for families	480,811		From the first child	For children up to 3	
		Aid for large families	600	Universal	From the third child (large families)	Single payment for children 0 to 6 years old	

Region		Benefit	Amount	Coverage	Applies to	Duration	Leave
Basque Country	Yes	Birth / adoption of children	Single payment 1,100/year	Universal	Second child	5 years	
		Multiple births	Twins: 2,600/year 1,200/year	Universal	Third and following children	Up to 3 Up to 10	
			Triplets: 4,000/year 2,400/year	Universal	Third and following children	Up to 3 Up to 10	
			Quadruplets: 5,400/year 3,600/year	Universal	Third and following children	Up to 3 Up to 10	
			Quintuplets or more: Additional aid	Universal	Third and following children		
Navarre	Yes	Aid for families	330/month	Universal	From the second child	1 year	Leave for one of the parents
		Birth of children	330/month	Universal	From the Third child	3 years	Leave for one of the parents
			Single payment of 1,980	Universal	From the Third child	Single payment 1 year	Incompatible with the previous one
			72/month for twins	Universal	Twins		

Table 2.2 (Continued)

Autonomous Community	Does it offer direct aid?	Type of aid	Amount (euros)	Income limits (euros)	Children	Age limit (length of allowance)	Other conditions
		Multiple births	180/month for triplets	Universal	Triplets	Up to 3 years	
			240/month for quadruplets +	Universal	Quadruplets	Up to 3 years	
			60/month for quintuplets and more	Universal	Quintuplets or more	Up to 10 years	
		Monthly aid for large families per child under 18	360/year	$7 \times$ minimum int. salary (No. children $+ 3 \times$ MIS)	4		Children up to 18
					5–6		
		Aid for families with children out of the home for university studies	901.12/child	$10 \times$ MIS	7 or more		Children up to 18
				Universal			Children up to 18
							Two or more children studying away from home

Castilla-la Mancha	No	Mutiple births	90.15/month	Not more than 7.5 × amount of the current MIS	Two children	For 2 years
			180.30/month		Three children	For 3 years
		Monthly aid for each child born following the four	300.51/month		Four or more children	For 5 years
			Increase of 60.10		Five or more children	
		Monthly aid for large families per child under 18	360/year	5 × MIS (one or two children under 18)	Three or more children	Until the 18th birthday
				No. children + 3 × MIS (three to seven children under 18)		
				11 × MIS (more than eight children under 18)		

Table 2.2 (Continued)

Autonomous Community	Does it offer direct aid?	Type of aid	Amount (euros)	Income limits (euros)	Children	Age limit (length of allowance)	Other conditions
Murcia	Yes	Aid for large families	Undefined	Universal	From seven children		Evaluation commission amount of all aid: 120,202 (in 2001)
		Large families second category	Undefined	Universal	From ten children		
		Large families recognised as 'families of honor' by the government. multiple births	Undefined	Universal	From triplets		
		Triplets and more					

Andalusia	Yes	Aid for families	600/year	6×MIS (increasing for more than three members)	From the third child	Until they are 3 years of age	If there are other children under 3
		Multiple births	1,200	6×MIS (increasing for more than three members)	Two children	For 3 years	
			2,400		Three and four children		
			4,800		Five children and more		
Extremadura	No						
Valencia	Yes	Multiple births	Single payment 1,205	Universal			Triplets or more
Galicia	Yes	Family with children under 3	Single payment 300	Exempt from income tax declaration (2001)	Children under 3		

Table 2.2 (Continued)

Autonomous Community	Does it offer direct aid?	Type of aid	Amount (euros)	Income limits (euros)	Children	Age limit (length of allowance)	Other conditions
Madrid	No						
La Rioja	No						
Cantabria	Yes	Mothers with children under 3	100/month	Universal		Until the 3rd birthday	
Balearic Islands	No						
Asturias	No						

The United Kingdom, a country where ambitious poverty-eradication programmes have been set up and which is famous for the guarantees of its public health and assistance system, is not defined as directly interventionist as regards infrastructures and direct support for families, unless they are poor. However, it does achieve results very similar to Sweden, with 63 per cent of women working and a birth rate of 1.6 children per woman. The law stipulates 18 weeks of maternity leave paid at 46 per cent, and childcare guaranteed after the age of three years.

In Spain, it is more and more common to hear experts talking of the need for a family pact that brings together the different aids of the autonomous communities and avoids comparative problems among families, not so much due to the number of children or the income as to the place they live. The current situation is summed up in Table 2.2.

3
Women: Agents of Change?

'People who have good lives are those who go in search of
the circumstances they want, and if they do not find them,
they make them, they manufacture them.'

Bernard Shaw

'The greatest souls are capable of the greatest vices and the
greatest virtues.'

René Descartes

Having gone through the history of women and the situation of family
support in different countries, in this chapter and the following we
will fully enter into the contradictions and paradoxes in women as
agents of change, and the tensions existing between work and family.

As we said in the first chapter, the second half of the twentieth
century is the time of the *massive influx of women into the job market*.
Sociologists view this as the most important event of this period, due
to its repercussions on many other phenomena derived from or
linked to it, such as the changes in or re-adaptation of family roles,
the incorporation of mothers' jobs into household dynamics and, as a
result, the variations in the family structure and work relationships:

According to the former dean of IESE, Juan Antonio Pérez López, if
the twenty-first century works it will be because women will have
an ever greater participation in the organisation of society, which
is in a deplorable state, poorly conceived and withstanding the
consequences of a declining, absurd rationalism. However, this

50

mission can only be accepted by women if it does not lead to dehumanisation, if she does not lose her femininity, because women are the core of the family and the family is the basis of society.[1]

Women today have left the private sphere and are now actively present in all professions; however, both spheres, the private and the professional, are still absolutely removed from each other as two incompatible tasks, with serious consequences for the way in which men and women live together and for the structure of society throughout the world. Men and women continue to question their personal identity and their role in the family and society. The company model that women can help to set up from a truly humanistic view of reality is much more in accordance with what is demanded by current times. Therefore, companies that wish to remain competitive in the new millennium must nurture a culture based on the solid values inherent in the female concept of humanism.

One of the main ethical challenges of globalization, not to say the first, is to recover the harmony between the traditionally male world of competitiveness/productivity and the world of the family, a space of co-operation and solidarity, identified with female work. These two worlds, that of efficacy and that of fertility, are not excluding or exclusive spaces for either sex but are clearly complementary.

Female ambition consists precisely of wanting to and being able to experience work as a *value shared with other life interests, basically the family*. In this sense, women are able to play a *certain educational role with men and create an efficient, productive working culture far removed from work addiction*, and thus avoiding some of the modern vices of dedication to work above all:[2]

> Women are more productive due to our ability to be in several things at the same time...we are more practical, more co-operative, we get down to business more...meetings with my sales manager take fifteen minutes.
>
> (area manager, three children)

> Women have brought productivity into the working world because we manage our time better.
>
> (economist, 36, two children)

> What characterizes women is that they work to the end.
>
> (general manager, mother of seven)

One can be an agent of change in any place, all that is necessary is a proactive attitude, that is, to want and to have a desire to act. In this case, the social change that we wish to carry out must begin with the family, given that it is here where the most qualitatively important time of our life is consumed. This influence will later reach the company and civil society.

However, it is not sufficient to support the silent revolution of this gradual change of customs brought about by the culture of conciliation; it is also necessary to change certain policies. To do this, women supported by men must also be in the key posts where the implementation of such policies is decided, not only because the matter concerns them but also because their more flexible management style and their different way of seeing and evaluating reality will make it possible to open up to new forms of work organization.

Until now many women have been agents of change, have brought flexibility into companies on many occasions through the very force of the facts (motherhood, having dependent persons in their charge, etc.). Achievements have often been briefly attained with courage and at the expense of their own health, but we believe that it is fair that now measures should be taken formally, in a methodical, systematic way that accommodates these realities, without forgetting that female ambition is not always focused on reconciling both worlds, but on giving one priority when the circumstances and the wishes of women themselves so determine; such is the case of motherhood experienced exclusively for a time. This choice is not often understood when one has not yet been a mother or when one has not taken on care-taking functions (dependent people) within the family.

Women can be agents of change in companies because their contribution is specifically needed and required at times such as the present, which require greater *flexibility* and learning capacity in a *business environment with more horizontal, flatter structures*. On the other hand, as we will discuss later, the *management competencies most highly valued by companies*[3] include several for which women seem particularly well endowed: customer orientation, leadership, initiative, teamwork, honesty, communication, interfunctional orientation, time management . . .

What gets in the way of female ambition?

> They did not cover my maternity leave, so it is impossible for the culture of my company to be considered pro-family.
>
> > (28-year-old journalist)

> I have an appointment at my child's school and two doctor's visits pending. I don't know when I'm going to be able to go.
>
> > (consultant, 33)

> Although I am on maternity leave, I can work thanks to my PC, mobile phone and the Internet.
>
> > (marketing manager, 30)

> I'm sorry, I will have a sandwich at the office because I can leave earlier then . . . or at least I hope so.
>
> > (mother of three, 36)

Women need to be allowed to be what they are by fostering and fundamentally respecting their motherhood, as the case may be, and then, as in the case of men, having their time after work respected, which is so essential and necessary to be able to recover and face a new working day, to be able to attend their family obligations and personal life. According to the study[4] of female Spanish managers through questionnaires and personal interviews, we are able to more precisely determine the *ten barriers* women have to overcome to achieve this.

1 Difficulties in reconciling family and working life

Asked the question, 'What criteria are important for you when taking decisions on your professional career?' two-thirds of women said that it was to achieve a balance between personal/family and professional life. The level of interest of a new job remains below that of the family when taking the decision in more than half of the cases; only for a third are the possibilities for promotion very important. Even among male managers,[5] the first criterion of choice when faced with different job offers is continuing to learn and, equally important, being able to have a life outside work. Remuneration only appears in third place.

These are data that agree with those of the Catenon Consultancy made on the basis of 600 Spanish workers (2003): three of every four Spaniards ask for a flexible work timetable and nine out of every ten would be willing to give up between 10 and 40 per cent of their salary to increase their quality of life with measures such as open working hours, the reduction of the working day or the possibility of leaves of absence:

> This company change has been brought on by the need to reconcile work and family. They offered greater flexibility and I have far fewer people under me. In exchange, I am able to take my children to school. A short time ago my son, proud of the fact that I took him there, introduced me to his teacher saying, 'Look, I have also got a mother.' When I worked in the multinational, I left home at 8 o'clock in the morning and when I got back they were already asleep.
>
> (area manager, married, 38, three children)

> After trying to combine a managerial post and my family and not achieving it, basically due to the lack of understanding in my company, I talked to my boss and I sort of gave in. Now I am there as an 'expert', which is the lowest level, but with a full-time, continuous working day outside the collective agreement, because if I go under the agreement they would not even recognize my university degree, which would be too much. I am very happy with change in terms of my family life, but I handle the content of my work very easily and quickly; it is too easy. I still report to an area manager and have strategy projects, but I have more capacity for work than what I have taken on and at the same time what I do lies outside the design of my post. They wanted to give me an assistant, but I asked them not to. What's more, I don't want to have anybody under me, and I'll carry on for another three years renewing my contract each year and then we'll see. In the end, I am expensive for the company. The work no longer motivates me as much, but that is what the company wanted. This is what my husband was worried about, that I would get depressed at having a job with little content. Now I feel more balanced personally, though not professionally satisfied.
>
> (female manager, married, 35, two children)

2 Lack of job flexibility

Women generally feel that they give more than they receive in the professional world. There is no lack of professional ambition (they rarely leave their jobs), or self-confidence (success is basically attributed to personal effort), but there is a certain implicit criticism of the absence of help from the state, from the company and from the hierarchical superior in his role as a mentor.

Women are also creative when resolving the work–family conflict when one arises and it cannot be solved in the company where they work. Sixty per cent move to another company, 27 per cent create their own company and, finally, 12 per cent become self-employed.[6]

Only 3 per cent take leave and 5 per cent reduce their working hours. According to the same study, 15 per cent give up work permanently to look after their children, and 22 per cent do so temporarily. These figures should change in the future with changes in legislation. It should be normal for women to take a leave of absence until their children are three years of age, or that they should work fewer hours until the children are six, as provided by law, if this is their wish or need.

In the United Kingdom,[7] two-thirds of mothers under 35 years of age would prefer to spend more time at home. A quarter of the women interviewed said that they preferred not to work while the father worked full time; 38 per cent believed that the ideal situation is that the father should work full time and the mother part time.

In fact another study, in this case by the Whirlpool Foundation,[8] reveals that the countries where women have entered the job market in great numbers are those least in favour of women devoting all their time to their professional career, which believe that they should be able to remain at home while their children are young, with better working conditions. Figures for Spain, however, show the opposite, perhaps because we have not yet come full circle like the countries mentioned in the survey. Spain is one of the countries with the lowest female employment rates, so women and society in general view favourably women entering 'outside' work. Yes, but . . . at what price and in what way?

When they reach a managerial level, women are able to value the future output of a good professional profile and take chances on people, even if they are pregnant:

Women are different. We do not see the sex, only the profile. I remember one of the employees that I hired to run a theme-based channel: she was pregnant and had had cancer, but she was the best. It was a complete success, even though the decision had been firmly opposed by the president.

(managing director, mother of three daughters)

Even when presented with the greatest professional opportunities, the experience of motherhood makes them change their viewpoint:

Do I have to put what is known as a professional career (so impressive and so fleeting) above building a good relationship with my daughter or my friends? Do we have to think first of rising professionally instead of living a meaningful life? Do I have to place the interests of the company before my own interests? The truth is that I don't think I want to. If (some) men are in favour of regaining sensitivity and feelings, they are welcome, because we will all win in the end. But I fear the superwoman of women's magazines, so efficient and dedicated, prepared to do a thousand things at the same time in order not to miss the boat (What boat? Where is it taking her?). My daughter, who trusts women more than men (sometimes I wonder whether I have gone too far in instilling self-confidence in her), is determined for me to be a boss because she still believes her mother is the best. I reply that bosses get home late, have meetings late in the afternoon because it is assumed that they do not have a private life, and often relinquish their own opinions to follow general directives. They are not free to decide what they think and sometimes have to flatter, etc. The truth is that I do not envy their position. I know that this is not always the case and that it is possible to do a responsible, creative job that is personally satisfying, even in managerial posts. But it is a scene that I have seen too often, and I am not interested in jumping on this wagon.

(regional manager of a service company, one daughter)

The truth is that when a woman does not mind being a woman and feeling like a woman with all its consequences, she can become a true agent of change. Men are fearful of us because we replace formal power with informal...and because we prefer personal fulfilment to success.

(intervention by businesswoman Mercedes Paniker in the global summit held in Barcelona in June 2002)

However, as a result of the extremely competitive circumstances of the working world, in our study almost no women in are in favour of reducing the working day for female managers:

Flexibility measures are harmful because they are for women and in the end they devalue us in the job market with respect to businessmen. What must be done is to reinforce the public services and aid policies. I would like the state to oblige men to stay with their children the same amount of time as their wives do.

(consultancy partner, married, 45, one daughter)

Although there are exceptions:

I was hired by a woman. I had been very burnt out in a new technology company. When my second child was born I asked for my working day to be reduced to six hours and it worked. From the start, she set the objectives, not the timetable. I think that if you demand flexibility you must also give it. I am available on my mobile phone and by electronic mail.

(human resource manager of a software company for Spain and Portugal)

3 Stress

Women do not take leave of absence, but they end up getting ill, this is the paradox. The survey reveals that 65 per cent of leave of absence amongst female managers is for this reason, in contrast to the rest of the female working population. Female managers have higher levels of stress and therefore are more liable to suffer cardiovascular illnesses than other professional women. The truth is that 80 per cent of Spanish women suffer from work-related stress,[9] in other words, due to the tension they suffer at work. The main group affected are women.[10] In Spain, women suffer more often from depression than men (9.2 per cent of women as opposed to 3.7 per cent of men):

When I was on leave, I considered reducing my working day and they told me they agreed. To show that I was interested, I reduced my holiday time and also my maternity leave and I managed to maintain my reduced timetable from then on. I am not sorry I did it, but I have paid in terms of promotion and sometimes in consideration. In the company, I was not set aside and continued to progress, I was overloaded, I was tired and I think this affected my son, who is very nervous. In any case I think I was valued there because it was a very small company. I worked a little at night and then I called the New York Stock Exchange before it closed. The company asked more and more of me without actually saying anything, it was very hard and in the end when my third child was born I left. That was three years ago. I have suffered from stress, in my first job I ate in fifteen minutes and felt that my heart was going to give out, but my boss was especially to blame. In any case, it is good to get some space away from work to see it from another point of view.

(investment fund manager, married, 32)

4 Long working days and double working days

Almost all female managers work outside the home eight hours or more and feel very satisfied (85 per cent) with their family life; however, two-thirds of them say they feel 'divided by a double workday'. Despite this, they make no formal criticism of the situation; they do not believe they are taking care of their family alone nor do they accuse their husbands or work companions of not giving them much support in this situation. It is obvious that professional women assume that achieving harmony between the two domains as a basically personal matter. Only 20 per cent of them say they feel that their husband 'is a burden'.

Although they value their private life, this attitude is not always accompanied by a proportional time dedication. Work comes in third place in their table of priorities; however, in practice it comes first. One only has to see the number of hours a day devoted to work in relation to the family. The same interpretation may be given to many other areas: children, husband, friends, etc. In other words, the values are defended but in practice time is taken up with other things.

As we shall see later, the use of our time defines us because the use of time is nothing more than a person's priorities made reality. We spend our time on what is truly important to us. In the relationship between work and family, the professional world clearly comes out on top at least concerning the number of hours put in during the week. Although the times probably overlap, what is striking is the importance of the number of hours each day devoted to 'my commitment to the company' (an average of eight hours a day), 'my professional plans' (four hours), 'the relationship with my companions' (two hours) and 'the relationship with my boss' (one hour), as opposed to the number of hours devoted to children (two hours) and husband (one hour). This imbalance appears to be compensated to a certain extent at weekends, but on many occasions this ends up being an area of co-existence characterized by rushing to and fro. In fact, it would be much better to fulfil the working hours during the week than to stop working Friday afternoons basically for two reasons: to respect the life cycle of living with the children every day, and to get used to living in ordinary situations. Otherwise, when the areas of co-existence are concentrated during the weekend, the family can only share fun and not difficulties or school homework, which are dealt with by babysitters or grandparents. Companies should be sensitive to taking care of flexibility in this sense. An extreme case in this area is children of parents who are separated: as the weekends are shared alternately between the father and the mother, co-existence may be defined more as 'artificial' or 'extra' time.

5 Little access to information and male network of contacts

As is highlighted by the North American researcher Mary Anne Devanna, 'as we move in a world run by men, women are excluded from the informal power networks, deprived of privileged information, poorly prepared for the games and strategies of company policies which condition access to the management posts':

> When I began to work, I even enjoyed certain advantages as the only woman. I went to the company's mixed commissions and often sat next to the president. At the beginning, maybe the first three seconds of meeting, they might think that you are mere adornment, but then they change their opinion when they see you work.

I thought it was a great opportunity to get to know a large company, but then you realize that you never know very well on what basis the decisions are taken and it makes you feel a little dizzy.
(self-employed businesswoman, married, 50, two children)

The first conflict came when they appointed me supervisor of a colleague. I said that we would talk about it, but he left as soon as he could, after two years. He wanted my post but I had got it, I must say I was just offered it without going after it. Why did a woman like me with such a global, strategic vision typical of general management not move in higher echelons? The reason I did not move up to higher levels is because I do not like battles and confrontations, I have only used my professionalism in the company. When a manager goes to another country it is very difficult for them to return, first because there are many others who want the post and then because, depending on your profile, nobody wants you below them because you're perceived as a threat, even though you might not be.
(vice-president of a multinational, 40, single)

Yes, men are frightened of hiring women managers. I tell you now I'm thirty-eight and pregnant with my third child and I have been regional manager of the company where seventy people reported to me and where I had six male managers as subordinates. Maybe as an excuse they will tell you that they are worried that women will not become involved (travelling, working from eight to eight) but in fact what they really fear is their management style and the fact that this might create conflicts not so much because they have men under them but because the managers on the same level as the woman do not accept her. The most conflictive situation in my career was when a colleague tried to take my post from me without being ready for it. It was the same person who replaced me four years later when I left to go to a consultancy. If you're in the minority and you come to a meeting they ask you to bring the coffee or take the minutes.
(area manager, married, 38, three children)

Lacking access to informal communication contacts, women find it more difficult than men to benefit from the support of mentors and sponsors, who are generally male. Some time ago the connection between professional success and mentoring was revealed; in the 1970s, two out of every three managers in large American companies acknowledged that they had been backed at least by one mentor, the result of which had mainly been to give them a higher salary in less time.[11]

Mentoring, tutoring or help from a professional who, in addition to being a manager, directs or accompanies the professional career of an employee, though unusual in Spain, has very positive effects:

> I studied agricultural engineering and when I finished, I had a grant to go to Holland without any clear mission. Then by chance I entered a consultancy hiring process. I had a training period in United States and later working in banks and putting in a lot of hours with a very young team, but since I enjoyed it I hardly got tired. The time I was in Chicago I found out what it was to work in a company with a clear mission and objectives and where everything was smoothly communicated. Promotion came fast. I got married at twenty-five after three years of engagement. He is a technical engineer and worked for an irrigation company. We went to live near the sea and after three years my first child was born; the company took it well.
>
> My best mentor was my manager at the time: he had had his first child just before me although he was considerably older. He helped me and paved the way for me. The advantage is that in a consultancy, work comes by projects. I tried to leave everything underway and delegated, and the contact I had with the customer also understood me very well.
>
> After four months of maternity leave, I asked for a reduction in my working day for another four months. They looked for a project adapted to what I wanted but it is difficult to run a team when you leave at 3 o'clock in the afternoon. I was assigned a training project in an important platform on a subject I knew nothing about. I studied while my daughter was in the park. Now I realize that it would have been better to work full time in the job I knew something about. I got over the situation thanks to the way I faced the subject, as I was more interested in knowing the people and the names than perfectly transmitting all my knowledge. My mistake

was not being able to say no and I allowed another person to decide for me. I went through a crisis and almost decided to stop working. I talked to my husband and a friend of his and reconsidered. I went back to work but all the timetables were incompatible with family life. I wanted to have more children, four years went by and my second child arrived. Then I was on another project but it didn't even occur to me to ask for a half-day. My oldest child was jealous; I had been in the company for seven years and as I had accumulated holidays we agreed that I could return gradually; by then I was a manager.

I was lucky to find another mentor; one of the partners in the company. He had a family vision: a wife and three children. He made it clear to me that it wasn't important if I was not promoted and did not develop my career fast.

(department manager, 36, two children)

Bearing in mind that human beings tend to select personnel similar to themselves, it is easy to deduce that there is a veto by men on women reaching certain levels of the company, which is very often subconscious and not the result of a clear desire *to structure power in this way*:

The problem of women managers does not lie with subordinates but rather with those on the same level or the general manager. In my case, my general manager is fearful of large projects and I have learnt to show him the cards little by little. We do not like to be problematic, conflictive, or stand out above the merits of the general manager, and even less so to contradict him. We avoid extra-professional criteria for promotion, we are frightened of it.

(manager at a service company, 45, separated, two daughters)

The truth is that in Spain only 4 per cent of the chairs on boards of directors are occupied by women. Maybe women are less available on these levels, but we should ask ourselves why. Perhaps companies are not very flexible and oblige them to drastically choose between promotion and family. In any case, women should be on boards of directors for many reasons, one of a very practical order: more than 50 per cent of consumer decisions fall upon them.

6 Lack of support

When it comes to evaluating the factors that have had an influence on professional success, only 10 per cent consider that a mentor has had influence on their career. This percentage rises to 42 per cent when we talk about emotional and educational support from the boss or colleagues. Generally speaking, the study gives higher percentages with respect to the subjective factors that have affected this same success: dedication (70 per cent), training (60 per cent), personality (50 per cent) and personal values (48 per cent). Husbands, professional strategy and the network of contacts barely accounted for 10 per cent.

It is clear that women experience their careers and professional promotions alone. Although they generally acknowledge that there are few company policies and that there is little support from the bosses in these matters, they also feel reticence at the implementation of services by some industrial complexes: 'I don't know if what they want is that, since I have a child in a nursery open twenty-four hours a day, I can work more time...'

7 Salary differences

When talking about salaries, a variety of aspects are included such as wages, promotion, stability, conditions and access to posts of responsibility. According to a survey made by the CIS,[12] 45 per cent of Spaniards believe that job inequalities between men and women are quite large. These data are confirmed by other studies,[13] according to which women are paid 27 per cent less for the same job, and the lower the university qualifications of the woman the greater the salary difference. Other international bodies[14] confirm this: Spanish female workers earn between 27 and 28 per cent less than men for the same job, whereas in the rest of the European Union this percentage falls to 15 per cent.[15] In Spain, the Ministry for Social Affairs has published a national action plan which will be carried out by work and social security inspectors in order to raise the awareness of businessmen and workers on this matter, and they have promised to draw up quarterly reports. This action plan has a budget of almost €3 million, jointly financed by the European Social Fund.

In fact, opinions on this matter are diverse: 'Spain is a country of SMEs, and this is an issue that is negotiated individually more than at managerial levels', some say. 'Women accept lower salaries', others explain with resignation. 'It is not a question of egalitarianism, but rather of fairness. To give to everyone what he or she deserves. Depending on what you want or can give, this is what you should receive. This also means being able to assume that flexibility has a price,' the majority conclude.

8   Little training in time management

This is one of the great pending matters. Only 30 per cent of those surveyed give any importance to this competence, even though it is one of the most important in successfully handling the work–family conflict from an individual standpoint. Although most women prioritize and make good use of their time, they are not satisfied with the results. The feeling of not getting round to everything is usual.

9   Difficulties in finding logistical support at home

Most of those interviewed also recognized that most stress does not come from the volume of work but rather from the pressure in this realm. Things change, but it is still the women who most strongly feel the weight and responsibility of the home. On this point, the percentage rises sharply. For 70 per cent of female managers, it is essential to have household help or have this matter resolved.

It is important to highlight that men do not fulfil their roles logistically, although they do emotionally. Only 32 per cent of couples in Spain equally share the housework. Women spend an average 4.2 hours a day on these chores, whereas men spend an average thirty minutes.[16] According to one of the interviewees, 'When men help they usually look for recognition for what they do. It is very difficult for sharing housework to be effective; they see it as a favour, not their responsibility.' In short, they think it is more a question of *helping* their wives rather than *sharing* the work and responsibility in the home and the care of the children and dependent elderly:

> In my opinion, what professional women need, and especially female managers who wish to be mothers and good professionals and happy wives at the same time, is a husband who supports them 100 per cent, a man capable of understanding the function performed by his wife, who enjoys her successes as if they were his own. Women, like men, need to come home and be happy.
>
> (businesswoman in the industrial sector, married, no children)

The importance of grandparents as an infrastructure of stability is so great that in the event of a change in managerial work, women do not consult their husbands but their mothers, as they need to know their specific availability for jobs such as picking up the children from school, staying with them while they do their homework or even putting them to bed at night.

In fact when women complain of a lack of personal time for themselves, their husbands' reproach is usually, 'you mean more time for us'. The truth is that time is spent between work, house and the children almost unwittingly and although in general women admit that there is harmony with their husband, they feel they have more logistical support from their parents.

Furthermore, this is clearly a significant source of employment, a focal point of emerging professions that has not been fully recognized from all points of view. Household staff require training and recognition of their work. Therefore, it is essential that they integrate into the family and form a strong core, a team with the mother or wife who is the person who organizes the home, even though she might delegate such tasks to these professionals. Household work is fundamental, its importance is not only material, but also emotional and spiritual. It embodies care and love for people. However, the experience is not good if child-rearing is 'abdicated' to the help:

Being self-employed has allowed me to take better care of my children. A housemaid does not have a child-rearing role, however, she sometimes ends up performing one because we are not there; grandparents partly manage to cover this gap; however, we sometimes forget that it is almost more important to be there in the pre-adolescence years. All good recipes on managing time, so useful in professional work, are only partly useful when talking about relationships with our children, which cannot always be scheduled. Children are unpredictable; you take them to school ninety days and there is no problem for eighty-seven, but one day there is a problem and this day they do not come to you to talk, because children do not call meetings. A lot is said about 'quality time' as the solution for mothers who work, but I don't agree; a lot of time is needed. Moreover, children (as is the case with one of my children) need more moral support than anything else. I would say that my son and I get good marks together; Ana, on the other hand, is more independent. Things are as they are.

(self-employed businesswoman, 50, two children)

10   Geographical mobility: an extreme situation of conciliation

Promotion often involves more travel or even a move to a new city or country. In such cases, women generally think of their husband or their children's schools, of their parents and their friends. Other times we get unexpected reactions. This is the case of a female manager whose husband was working in Germany when she was working in Madrid:

My boss talked to me about a hypothetical promotion in London. 'I didn't say anything to you because as you have your daughter...' he began. I said I was interested. In the end it was something that I would not have been able to do if we had been together. From London we continued to see each other periodically, even more often than when I was in Madrid.

(Director of a multinational company, one daughter)

The glass ceiling

The so-called 'glass ceiling' is a series of unwritten rules that are in the company culture and prevent women from reaching the top. Until now we have seen the family, personal and marital circumstances that have an influence on the career of a professional woman. But what about the company structure? To what extent are women allowed to be present at the key points?

Obviously the management of people in the twenty-first century will require a less hierarchical, more flexible and empathic style, with an ability to listen which generates and facilitates teamwork. All of this is what has been called 'the female management style'. Before, such features were associated with a lack of authority because the overriding tendency was 'order and control', the *manu militari*. Changing the prevailing direction means that the company is taking a step forward and thus adapting to a different style of employee, generally more mature. Today we are at a time of collision between the two prevailing management currents: both kinds of companies co-exist, but with the difference that today women are not only ready for change (in the past the company structure prevented this and many adopted a male role which worked against them in the long run), but also corporate sensitivity and the environment make it easier for them.

The establishment of policies and the institutional support causing a change in the working climate will always come from the management posts; therefore, there must be enough women in these echelons. The possibility of their being an agent of change exists, but the sheer number of women also counts and unfortunately today they are in a minority in the top posts. According to the study conducted by Women Directors International,[17] *only 24 per cent of the 300 Spanish companies with the highest income have any women on their boards of directors.* In absolute numbers, of the 2,486 board members in these companies, only 115 (4.6 per cent) are women. Even more specifically, on the IBEX 35, which lists the largest Spanish companies quoting on the stock exchange, there are only fifteen women of a total 400 board members. As regards management posts, including those with a certain degree technical expertise, only 25 per cent of them are held by women.[18] What do these figures mean? They mean that as long as this continues, the desired, required change is not feasible.

Without a critical mass and without participation in the power centres where the decisions are taken, the way of doing business will not change. It is highly improbable that the female point of view and decision-making criteria will be heeded or included in company policies and strategies. In almost 50 per cent of cases, power in companies is accessed through merit and the contact network. The rest of the working world (public administration, universities, middle school teaching, freelance professions and so forth) are more balanced, with women far better represented and more equal on all levels (perhaps mainly due to the fact that access routes – merit, examination – are more 'democratic' and objective).

The scarce representation of women in managerial posts[19] is the main *obstacle* to their *professional development.* Furthermore, their limited presence in these key places is the reason why they have few role models to look towards. The second obstacle is the rigid, hierarchical management style of some bosses.

Despite the feminization of university degrees, and despite the unacceptability of chauvinism, despite the promotion of a kind of female leadership in some sectors, hardly anything has changed in terms of the presence of women in the centres of corporate decision-making. Corporations, centres of economic power, Chambers of Commerce and management associations are in the hands of men, as are sales networks, business opportunities and privileged information on these areas, which include encouragement to export.[20]

We know that there are *entry barriers* prior to hiring.[21] A young woman who has recently earned a master's degree, with solid preparation and experience will find it difficult to be hired if she declares that she intends to start a family and make it compatible with her professional life.

It can also occur that, once inside, she will suffer from *internal barriers to promotion*, especially if her career falls in with the traditional model: linear, incessant promotion. This attempt at continual vertical progress goes against the natural cycle of a woman's motherhood. Statistics say that in the year 2001, the average age for giving birth for the first time was thirty-one, which means that a woman's career high point usually coincides with their period of maximum fertility. In light of this, companies should bear in mind the possible lack of continuity in women's professional careers not as an obstacle or delay, but also as a legitimate option. Why do we not consider the development of a professional possible at thirty-five or forty after a period of leave or a professional plateau? Remaining on a professional plateau for several years or taking a leave does not mean bidding farewell to working life, and much less so today with the new technologies that allow us to be in constant contact with the significant issues inside and outside the company:

> In any case, it is a social failure for women to give up being mothers for their work.
>
> (Maria Victoria Camps, a talk given on 24th April 2003 in the student residence in Madrid)

For me, the best option is to receive training, then form a family and then be more intensely devoted to one's profession. I took a five-year break to look after my children, even though I had an extraordinary husband. Anyone who puts off marriage to become established professionally suffers more acutely later, because they are higher up in the company and feel they have less strength to give up if they have to do so. One must be capable of taking free, responsible decisions at the beginning of one's career. It is not enough to design one's career, we must also try to predict our lives, otherwise problems appear suddenly and often dramatically for intelligent, competent women because, despite having overcome all the other barriers in their professional lives, family life eludes them.

(graphic design team leader, three children)

In any case, women need the co-operation and support of their husbands; they must make decisions like a true team, in the professional arena as well. 'I'll forge ahead now and you slow down...'

I only took four days of maternity leave, it was impossible to do anything else. At that time my husband could spend more time with our daughter and did so. When I had the twins one year later, it was the other way round.

(financial manager, married, 35, three children)

... and the cement ceiling

'But exploding the glass ceiling would not happen from the goodwill of managers, rather the determination of women to assault on the top of the pyramid', Candy Deemer reminds us.[22] In addition to the glass ceiling that some have managed to break with their 'assault on the top', there are also barriers within women. This is what we call the 'cement ceiling', which nothing or nobody can break because it has been deliberately self-imposed by women themselves. In such cases, women reject all kinds of promotion, seeing the difficulties that they might find in a new post in reconciling work and family life or fleeing from the struggles and manipulations of a primarily masculine world where they can sometimes feel very alone. This situation can be found particularly amongst women in systematized, controlling companies with a short-term vision and long working days at the office.

The reaction is then to avoid the formal power offered due to the personal and family cost that it would incur in terms of time and quality of life. They thus prefer to continue working from influence or informal power, in short, a different way of directing their ambitions.

In the case of women with children, they see their career is held up not only because they ask for leave but also because they take the entire maternity leave due to them. This decision can become an issue with their bosses and mark the beginning of workplace reprisals, which are unfair, tacit and sometimes invisible, yet real. In the cases we cite below, there is a combination of the glass ceiling and a cement ceiling where women anticipate the consequences:

> In September, after six months [since the birth] I went in with a permanent contract. I know that professionally speaking it wasn't the best decision. I was in a position where I could move up; it was a time when I was going to be involved in a much better project, it was like moving up inside the company, but I chose to give up a rapid advance and devote the first years of my child's life to the family. I am very happy, but the work is not the same. You don't do as interesting things as you could, because they don't give you major projects. But I am not the typical gal with very high aspirations. Another woman in the same situation would be unhappy. What I want is for my job to be my second world.
>
> (departmental manager, married with two children)

In this case, the decision was premeditated; the decision had already been taken before any hypothetical promotion could appear. Other times, the decision is the result of weighing what one has, what one could be and what one could lose:

> I studied economics and business and then did a master's degree. There I met my future husband. I decided to look for work in Barcelona and began to work in a financial services company. After three years there and two being married, my first daughter arrived. As soon as I married I had a crisis; work no longer motivated me and I considered giving it up. I think the real reason was the person who was my boss; women need to work with people they like, but men ignore all of this. Everything changed when I went to another department that was more oriented towards providing services to companies, assessments, investment fund analyses, and I stayed there for twelve years.
>
> When my second child was born and the oldest one was four years old, they offered me a very important promotion, but I would

have had to work full time. I talked to my husband and he backed me. I talked to my father-in-law and he felt that it would be easy with suitable help at home. I feared for my marriage and he told me that in that case first things first, and I turned down the promotion.

(market analyst, two children)

In other cases, family life is not the reason for the decision; it is more a premeditated decision not to fight for formal power:

After a short time, my boss got lung cancer. It was a hard year not only because he wasn't working as hard and died in the end, but because it triggered a series of internal conflicts in the company, and although the post naturally was mine, I did not fight for it. Another person from outside Spain wanted it and got it: a woman with a desire for power. She did not speak Spanish, she did not know the market, and therefore, looking at the situation from the outside, everything seemed to be in my favour: relationships with the businesses, ministry, suppliers, etc. Before, she had constantly ignored my functions, and she also felt jealous of the informal power I had over people, as I had hired and trained most of them in the past eight years. Finally, this person confronted my boss, the vice-president of the company for Europe, and left. She failed, but it affected me because I lost the opportunity to gain her post. At the time, I was working in France and they wanted me to go to another city, Spain had already been requested by another controller.

(multinational vice-president, 40, single)

A recent study conducted in the United Kingdom indicates that one in every three women working outside the home has at some time rejected a possible promotion or further training in favour of their family.[23] The report, which coined the term 'familyism' to describe the predominant factor that prevents women from accepting managerial positions, suggests that in addition to the inequality with which companies usually treat their executives, the truth is that many of them decide to put their children and their home first.

Most of the 1,000 women surveyed admitted that the pressures between family and work are very intense. Many of them declared their despair at needing a 26-hour day to be able to fulfil all of their commitments. Nearly 60 per cent of women between 30 and 55 responded that the relationship with their partner and children would improve with these extra two hours a day. More than half added that their personal happiness would also be greater with two hours more free time.

The results of the study also cast doubt on the policies in favour of the family that many companies have begun to introduce, according to Bola Olabisi, founder and manager of the Professional Family Woman's Network and mother of four children. 'Many businessmen, particularly in large companies, have policies that look impressive on paper. But when will the time come when managers understand them and put them into practice? That is another story.' She adds, 'Companies need to understand the wide variety of unused resources that are lost it simply because they do not recognize the valuable contribution of mothers in the workplace.'

In a working environment where women managers are in the minority, businessmen behave as though we were in the 1950s, when most workers were men and their family responsibilities were covered by their wives, who remained at home. With this stuck attitude, they harm themselves and the company because they ignore reality, which is not a very suitable way to operate.

Some women get to the top, but they do not stay there for long. According to the French sociologist and writer, Gilles Lipovetsky,[24] the reasons might be associated with these women's loneliness in a male world. Men defend themselves by saying that power is privilege of the male sex, and they associate the stereotypes of professional success with the qualities usually attributed to men. Women are still considered excessively emotional, not fighters, poorly adapted to managing production units, less capable of having a spirit of initiative and less involved in the company. They also generally receive less *feedback* on their work performance, as men find it more difficult to judge their efforts.

This may be an explanation for why women are present above all in departments that support the company (human resources, communication, computer science, planning, marketing, finance) and far less in operational functions (production, sales), which are more closely associated with male qualities (energy, combativeness, decision-making, total commitment).

Some women also seem to have a fear of being visible. This is the typical attitude of minorities. Women have a tendency to withdraw, to hide, a tendency that is not fear of success but rather a fear of being judged for it, something as serious for a manager as stage fright for a politician; no matter how good they are, they will be condemned to always remain in the background.

Female values: more humane companies?

Men's tendency to regard the world impersonally through logical and legal systems, as opposed to the way women do it, through a series of relationships moved by human connections more than rules, means that we can talk of a special way of looking at the world.[25] It is possible to reach similar judgements with these differing perspectives, but the different visions, decision-making processes or starting points of the problem enrich both parties and, obviously, the company in its overall vision of reality. It was precisely at the 4th International Women's Conference in Beijing in 1995 that the same idea was postulated, developed and concluded: the world must be viewed through the eyes of a woman to thus complete the vision of reality that has been perceived for centuries and through which humanity's social life has been organized.

What does this mean in practice? Naturally, and the figures attest to this, there are no differences in intellectual capacities and nor in inclinations towards certain areas of knowledge, such as the sciences or arts (the traditional division now no longer in use). However, it is possible to talk about different ways of learning, different ways of solving problems, different ways of relating and maybe a different way of experiencing certain values or developing certain competences that reflect values in action.

In companies, *it is necessary to blend rationality and affective factors* and to balance rational and intuitive systems in management. This involves 're-conceiving companies' as a whole, among men and women, to make them more friendly, more humane, more flexible and more efficient:

> In the working world, men do not accept claims that are not based on figures and data. I 'see' many things, it is pure intuition, but I have to find data to be able to back what I say, because if not I lose value.
>
> (investment fund manager, married, 32, one daughter)

One of the skills currently most highly valued in an organization is *creativity*. One way of nurturing it is to be capable of seeing things from different points of view. When there are problems, challenges, issues to be resolved, there is no ideal solution, since there is usually more than one way to do things. Therefore, having different ways of perceiving, handling and resolving problems enriches the company and its overall functioning by contributing their femininity in the different stages of the problem-solving process.

The preponderance of abstract knowledge in men and experiential knowledge in women lead to different ways of approaching decision-making. Men are very good at finding alternatives; women, at evaluating these alternative actions, in other words, at establishing criteria or parameters on the decision-making.

In general terms, the intuitive-inductive system more typical of female thought is particularly useful when decisions have to be taken with few quantitative data, based on experience and observation of reality and making comprehensive use of all rational and emotional data. However, when intuition is not backed by in-depth rational training and a certain degree of objectivity when considering the facts, it may give rise to more imaginary than real evaluations of reality that have nothing to do with heart-felt intuition that is in harmony with reason:

> We are only different from them in one thing: intuition, a quality we have. I do not know if this is through actual or potential motherhood, which makes us more capable of seeing people and taking the right decisions, but we are capable of foreseeing consequences that they do not see.
>
> (businesswoman, 50, three children)

Furthermore, recent studies on management styles[26] show that women as a group, despite theoretically preferring a rational system of decision-making in practice, especially when they hold higher positions in the organizational hierarchy, make greater use of intuition. In any case, we must bear in mind that whenever we generalize we can commit individual injustices as there will always be exceptions to the sociological rules. Studying the differences does not enable us to generalize, but to reveal predominant tendencies or traits in either sex. Let us examine the following:[27]

Men are more oriented towards power and status:

> In general, a man is more concerned with his status and this being
> visible. Women also want to achieve status, but not at the
> expense of others. This is where the concept of success comes in.
> Society is highly male-oriented, and this is why we have a very
> visible concept of success. When a woman enters this process, she
> automatically adopts a male role.
>
> (consultancy partner, mother of one daughter)

Women are more motivated by psychological factors and a desire for
self-realization:

> I believe that we approach our professional life wrong. Personal life
> has affirmations, which is what I want. Professional life contains
> what I do not want, and I am quite sure that I do not want to die of
> a heart attack or on a plane or in a hotel and keep getting up at
> 4 o'clock in the morning two days a week. I don't want to have
> depression, or stress, or to take drugs, or to distort my mood because
> I have needs that I do not fulfil, and this is something that I see in
> my colleagues who get to the top, but they have to pay this price.
>
> (manager of a pharmaceutical multinational, single, 40)

Female managers and businesswomen must make a greater effort and
be more harsh to be recognized; they suffer more pressure than men,
are more constantly subject to judgement, perhaps because they are
in a minority, because a woman is taken as a model for other women
and whenever one has a problem they say 'They're all the same',
which is not said so much of men, because women are more pessi-
mistic about their opportunities:

> We women more frequently come upon the often not-explicit dis-
> course that we should not be problematic or conflictive or stand out
> above the merits of the general manager, much less contradict him.
>
> (manager of a service company, mother of three
> daughters, separated)

In general, women find it more difficult to separate their feelings
from their work, which means that they take decisions involving

their whole personality. Plainly speaking, they continue to be more human than men, precisely because they are less compartmentalized in their way of thinking:[28]

> We never regard a person as useless for a role, we deal with the problem directly with them. Maybe this is why we hold so many positions of responsibility in human resources. It is sometimes said disparagingly that a woman is very much a mother in some areas, and I think this is good. If we are 'real' women (not women who have adopted a male role) we see the person as a whole with a less utilitarian view. This is also useful for the company in the long term. It is always important for a manager to be close to people, because the further you rise in the hierarchical ladder, the further you are from reality and the more you undertake your own race . . . but if you want everything to work, you must be on the side of people, truly understanding their circumstances.
>
> (investment analysis manager, 36, two children)

This has its negative side:

> We do not separate emotions from profession. A good friend is no longer one if they let you down at work. Men separate this much more. They are capable of being angry with the situation, with what you represent, with what you have done . . . but not with you yourself. It is as if women find it more difficult to forgive, to forget . . . We take work matters as personal attacks.
>
> (businesswoman, mother of three)

At other times it can enrich management:

> Productivity is not the only value that a woman takes into account when she is a manager, perhaps because we are naturally concerned with forming people. Life has taught me to be less of a perfectionist and to be more aware of people. Personally speaking, it has always been very useful for me to treat people better than they are so that they might improve.
>
> (manager of a service company, separated, mother of two daughters)

In addition to being very aware when taking decisions about people, women are more capable of finding effective, fair alternatives for conciliation:

> We are more human, we especially see the person with all their circumstances. They see more a person who has a job to do. I say this based on my own experience: how I treated a manager who asked for a shorter working day and how they treated me. I was separated, I stopped going to meetings, they ignored me completely before I left the department...In contrast, not only did I avoid all of this with my manager, but I also found him another position adapted to his circumstances without reducing his job category. I placed no conditions or doubts on his current and future output due to the fact that he wanted to devote part of his energy to his role as a father.
>
> (computer manager, 33, mother of one daughter)

The former dean of IESE, Juan Antonio Pérez López, talked about functional equality without losing femininity, and highlighted the executive efficiency of women. 'In companies it is generally said that the major decisions are strategic. I do not agree. Everybody has strategy, though not always expressed clearly enough. But the problem is generally one of implementation, and women are very good at this, at putting something into practice':[29]

> While men try to achieve their objectives in a more aggressive manner, we seek collaboration, persuasion, harmony. If they express their opinion with claims, women question things so that there might be a reflection on the way of doing it...We are equally efficient, but for women with children, time is a scarcer resource than for men and we make better use of it.
>
> (manager of a computer multinational, married, no children)

Women manage and work making use of their innate tendency towards interpersonal communication and are less likely to suffer from stress simply due to hormones, although it is true that they have recently begun to suffer more from stress due to their multiple obligations stemming from their effort to reconcile family and professional life.

If we want, women can be agents of change in a new culture of success, less associated with money and status and closer to inner growth, creativity and co-operation. We need the complicity of men capable of modifying the erroneous concepts of privileges that underlie a misunderstood masculinity.

If men were the agents of change in the industrial era, we are agents of change in the era of knowledge. However, women do not want to be the leaders of a dysfunctional system where there is a tremendous gap between what the world offers and what we need as people. How do we resolve this situation? How is it possible to reach the top (the top that each person aims for) and to change the structures at the same time? The best way is by becoming reference points about what we believe is the best.

Work undoubtedly contributes to our personal identity. However, women are less trapped by status, by calling cards, by the others' opinions of our career; we are capable of having a broader experience of success where one's life history includes work and family without breaks or exclusions, taking each facet at the right speed for the time we are experiencing. We are thus entering an exciting subject which we will develop in a later chapter: it is impossible to lead others if we are not capable of running our own lives. A good leader must also be capable of finding something positive each day in those who surround him, thus generating a climate of trust, solidarity and stable relationships. This is added value. This is the change.

In short, diversity requires new forms of organization which in no way will dilute the effectiveness of the results or the success of the organization, rather quite the opposite, they will enhance them. For the system to be good, it must serve one and all: 'The more difficult it is for women – for female persons – to be integrated in a social structure (company, state, province, municipality...), the more poorly designed the structure is, the more inhumane it is, the less effective it is and the more it harms everybody'.[30]

4

Work and Family: Can They be Reconciled?

'Love is the active concern for life and the growth of what we love.'

Erich Fromm

'Virtue is philosophy in action.'

Pythagoras

A life trajectory with a professional career

Family life helps us to be happy, but the concept of success is still related to something external and visible. This is why we continue to talk about 'careers' instead of 'professional trajectories' or 'life trajectories', a concept that views life as a whole where people are developed in different areas.

To talk about a 'trajectory' instead of a 'career' involves looking at life itself as something more than a professional plan carried out with the mentality of always running faster and faster against another person. But the fact is that we resist change also on an individual level. Many say that they long for the family or children they decided not to have or gave up as their price for rising professionally. Renunciations and accepted prices, decisions taken one day when a man or woman felt that the bow was becoming tense and about to break: work or family. Absorbing professional years or stages preventing quantitative and qualitative attention to the spouse and family, the absence of children for women who feel incapable of losing their place in the ranking or their chair on the board of directors, postures that ask the great question: family, a professional bonus or penalty?

If we analyse the problem only from the standpoint of the use and availability of personal time, it is true that the family may occasionally slow up a specific professional trajectory. But if we analyse the psychological states of many professionals resulting from the imbalance between these two factors, it is clear that reason is not enough for a human being, nor is having it all, when what is at stake is being happy and having a balanced life.

A personal life that encompasses not only the family, but also the world of relationships, friendships, motivations and one's degree of individual satisfaction is what determines and gives stability to a life as a whole. The heads of personnel departments perceive that the quality of relationships that a manager, a professional, sustains outside the company are decisive for them, for gaining the loyalty of the executive and for their equilibrium throughout their professional career.

Parents, spouses, professionals. Is there a priority role? This is the first dilemma. Living to work or working to live: this the second. Some parents who are also professionals have courageously begun to pose these questions and in doing so are toppling some stereotypes and along with them the fear of saying, 'I have a family.' The stereotype has been toppled that defined a good manager as one capable of giving up everything for work. In its place we can see the emergent idea that a person capable of successfully balancing the two most important spheres of his life, family and profession, is a truly effective manager with authentic leadership skills.

Dual-income couples: problems and perspectives

In the past twenty-five years in Spain, two million women have joined the ranks of the working world compared to 300,000 men. This massive influx of women in the job market means that a new social reality has appeared: dual-income couples.

In Spain, 64 per cent of families are made up of couples who work outside the home. This has repercussions in three areas: family, society and business. The most noteworthy characteristics of this new reality are seen in:

- An increase in the sources of income.
- The greater economic and legal independence of the parties in a marriage, especially the women.
- A change in the values and priorities brought about by the new workplace obligations.
- Greater stress due to the difficulty of reconciling work and family, especially for women.
- And finally, a fall in birth rates due in many cases to the difficulty of handling a pregnancy and child-rearing at the same time as the responsibilities of a paid professional job.

Although it is true that the entry of women in the working world has been important, it does not mean that men's and women's dedication and devotion to the family and to work have been the same. Couples in this situation, with two careers and long working days, also see their marital homes and their interpersonal relationship as being in jeopardy. Sometimes they see each other at most once a day, as opposed to the three traditional meals, breakfast, lunch and dinner, as in the past. Moreover, the spectre of rushing reduces spontaneous moments of relaxation, and it is more and more common for people to arrive home so exhausted they hardly have any energy for the home. It could be said that in terms of living together, the lack of time and the difficulty in changing roles (from executive to mother and wife) oblige women to 'get down to the nitty-gritty' and this attitude, undoubtedly very practical, may be dangerous when there are any types of problems, as attention is so fleeting that the problems might not even be noticed.

Conflicts between work and family[1] occur when there is a lack of planning, when there is very unequal involvement between the members of the couple in one of the two areas and there is a significant situation of overloading from the work to the family sphere or vice versa.

Three kinds of asynchronies may be given in these kinds of professionals.[2] First is the so-called 'organizational asynchrony' caused when the development of a person's career does not follow the 'normal' organizational rhythms or the generalized social expectations. The second is the so-called 'couple asynchrony' which involves the different professional careers of both spouses. This is where the 'I lose, you win' syndrome appears, in other words, the sensation that one of the two is giving up a sphere, the family in favour of work or the other way round, seeing that the other spouse is benefiting from more personal time, a better professional career. The last is 'family asynchrony', which is nothing more than a failure to create a family in accordance with social expectations or values: this involves the intentional, permanent absence of offspring.

With these premises, it is essential to know the distribution of roles and functions when diagnosing at what point the work–family harmony lies in a specific marriage. A number of situations may be given:

- *Established*: When each member is predominantly dedicated to one of the two life spheres, one to the family and the other to the profession
- *Allied*: When the two focus on the same sphere (either family or profession) and agree to ignore the other area that has been excluded
- *Adversaries*: When the exclusion of the other sphere is not the result of a mutual agreement and therefore gives rise to a search for someone to blame for what was not done
- *Balanced*: Those where both parties try in good faith to be present and take responsibility for both spheres (work and family) and as a result suffer a great deal of stress that can force them towards the adversary type.

With respect to the possibility of a change in trends in terms of the responsibility for housework, different studies agree that 50 per cent believe that both sexes will share the tasks of raising their children. Ninety per cent believe that men and women will shoulder the income and expenses of the household together, and 85 per cent of those surveyed are sure that there will be no return to traditional roles.

Families, and more specifically dual-income families, are today faced with new problems. First, problems in the couple:

- Less time spent together with the resulting paradox: money (increased income) cannot buy the time, which was precisely the privilege of the rich in another time
- Professional rivalry. Which of the two slows down their professional career when more time and energy must be devoted to the other family members?

Second, problems in the professional sphere itself:

- Due to the possible conflict between work and family, the career does not follow the expected trajectory
- Life itself is designed in terms of the choices taken in one's professional career plans. Families are not planned, and decisions are not taken with it in mind. The conflict comes later
- The family suffers the consequences of making career development the main priority. The increase in the divorce rate and the low birth rate are the initial consequences.

Finally, problems in the family:

- Conflict with respect to household work sharing and responsibilities in the home (a role exclusively taken on by the woman in the past).

The new situation obliges us to reconceive companies and the ways of organizing society between both, and the personal and social challenges that are posed are intriguing: first, the construction of both society and company by both the man and the woman; second, taking the demands of the family into the social, political and business realms; and, third, appearance of the new feminism of complementariness, thus overcoming post-feminism based on radical gender equality. This meant adopting the male role as a condition for the successful inclusion of women into the working world. The feminism of complementariness promotes the specific qualities of both men and women in the economy, society and family, in search of fairness. Fairness assumes equality and goes beyond it as a concept, as each one is given what they are due and also what they need according to their circumstances.

The family as a resource or problem

The family affects our work in different ways depending on whether we consider family life a resource or a problem.[3]

When viewed as a resource, what might take place is that one spouse may help by contributing income, in the professional self-realization of the other partner and in the organization of the family timetable, by giving the other partner significant personal support and thus increasing the level of family authority. Or the spouses might support each other mutually in their respective careers in order to increase their social life and network of personal contacts. Let's see some accounts of how the family has reinforced the working life of some women:

By learning from the family how to establish priorities and manage time

I think that in a certain way we have to ensure that each of these two areas, work and family, do not conflict with each other as though it were a competition but that they should rather understand and accept each other. We have to try to make sure that both the husband and the children feel part of a woman working out of the home, not only through the economic aspect this involves at the end of the month. Taking the little children to mummy's office from time to time, asking older children to read and requesting their opinions on the originals of some books before publishing them or simply telling one's husband about any incidents on the way to achieving the sales objective we have set; these are practical ideas which I think have worked for me.

This family–professional work duality has positive aspects that should be enhanced. For example, it helps you to forget yourself to attend to others. When you get in the lift in the morning to go to the office, you 'try' (I say 'try' because you cannot and do not wish to) to forget your child's fever that has kept you up all night. When you return home, you erase from your mind (this is easier) a customer who has not paid or the supplier who has not delivered. In this double game, you can get home at night and then discover that you haven't forgotten yourself. This is an effective formula.

I do not allow myself to become obsessed with having the house in perfect order, although it is obvious that this is necessary to make life pleasant for others, even in the physical sense. One of the few things that I remember my parents saying when I was young was that work had to be well done. And this is what I teach my children when they leave things unfinished as they are tidying up the table.

I have also learnt that a good manager is not the one who does the most, but rather the one who ensures that others do so, and as I believe that running a house is not very different from running a company, since in both cases we are managing human beings, I delegate much of the housework to my children and the cleaning lady.

It is very useful to organize household tasks in a pyramid of priorities. At the base is the housework: feeding, cleaning and maintenance. If this is done well we can say that the house 'works'. On the intermediate level are the jobs intended to make family life better: tidiness and decoration, health, leisure... these are all intended to create a pleasant environment, a home 'where one likes to be'. Finally, the top level includes communication with one's partner and the children's upbringing in both the intellectual and the humane and spiritual levels. Well, the further we go down the pyramid, the more we must delegate in order to have more time to devote to the higher, much more important jobs.

(managing director of a publishing house, three children)

Achieving personality balance through the multiple roles that are undertaken

I studied at a prestigious university. The atmosphere was very competitive. When they brought in some female director, for instance, the phrase was always the same, 'If you want to be something, you have to choose between family and work.' They were clear. However, I didn't really believe it, although I still wasn't very worried about it because I didn't have a boyfriend. Asked the question of where I imagined myself in five years' time, I never saw children; however, internally, like a distant desire, I knew I wanted to have them. I worked as an internal auditor in multinational companies and met interesting people, I made friends... I could have gone a long way there, but I met my future husband and changed my plans. When you have an inner life, your values find their place, you are incapable of becoming obsessed. I tend to get depressed and the only stages of my life when I do not take medication are during pregnancies and when I am breast-feeding. I have set up my own company, I have worked as a consultant, but I have realized that no challenge is comparable to bringing up your family.

I have learnt that family life also has its challenges. In the beginning, my attitude with the children was to get home and play with them, which is what working men also do. Now I realize that raising children is a significant challenge, and the children also realize this. When they see a boy throw things on the floor they say, 'Look mummy, that boy must always be with babysitters.' And the fact is that children need a timetable, you cannot forget about them one day and the following day put in time. What's more, they need you individually.

(businesswoman, mother of three children)

The good thing is that I am never bored! I think that one of the great advantages of being a working mother is the variety and the contrast in my life: I place a great deal of value on the change from the working day to the afternoon with my children, from the week to the weekend, and from the school year to the summer holidays. Above all, since I have had three children, I disconnect totally and absolutely at weekends. I dedicate 100 per cent of my time to them and on Monday when I go back to work, although it takes you a few minutes to remember what you were doing on Friday, you go back mentally fresher (though maybe physically tired). It is also nice to think and work in peace for a few hours. I don't know, but looking at it positively, I think we could be one of the most motivated working groups, simply because of the variety our obligations give us.

(Lawyer, 32, two children)

When the family is viewed as a problem, motherhood/fatherhood is seen as a damper on a professional career. What is more, 50 per cent of the women interviewed recognized that their work often prevents them from tending to their husbands better. In these cases, attention and output at work also fall, alterations in the working timetables are constant and frequent, professional aspirations are lowered and the career itself is frequently altered in line with family needs. In some cases, work even invades the family life:

I am an area manager at a financial entity, I am responsible for eighteen people and I used to work ten hours a day. When I came back after a maternity leave I was given more responsibility, an important project that required a lot of my energy. I ended up exhausted, stressed and under psychological treatment.

My son's illness was a shock for me that I did not assimilate very well. I am grateful that this did not happen when I was forty or fifty, but rather when I had just turned thirty. Now I have changed my chip, and I realize that you have to know your limitations at all times and know how far you can go.

When I got married, I had just changed companies. I did not have children for three years and since we both worked long hours, there was not really anything to reconcile. We cherished our times chatting at night even though we slept less, and also at the weekends. When the children came I immediately took them to the nursery, and although the truth is I did not see them very much, I knew they were well cared for. Since they went to bed late I was able to spend a lot of time with them. It is now that they are growing and beginning to ask questions that I wonder if they need me more.

My boss is a single man and has no sensitivity as far as timetables are concerned. I have managed to make him respect my Friday afternoons, but he is still impossible during the week. I'm not criticizing anything, the work has to be done but I don't know how to do it all. On the other hand, I do not think about the future. I have never thought of changing companies or giving up working, I don't consider it because I know I cannot economically and because I don't think I could put up with being at home. I like to live day-by-day in the present.

(financial manager, married, 35, two children)

The family: a school of competencies

Current hiring trends confirm that strong professional backgrounds are sought[4] both in all aspects related to intrategic skills or competencies (communication, people management, motivation, delegation, coaching, teamwork)[5], and the competencies of personal efficiency (initiative, creativity, optimism, time management, attention management, stress management, self-criticism, self-awareness, personal improvement, self-control, decision-making, emotional balance and integrity).

Practically all of these competencies are developed within the family and are then used in professional life. The family is a place where one gives and receives, the place where we all learn to give and sacrifice.

Every day, a mother develops competencies and management skills: the capacity to communicate on all levels (from the baby to the paediatrician) or negotiate (whether with the shopkeeper on the corner or the technicians who have to come repair a household appliance). She is constantly negotiating with her husband, with the household help, with her children... At the same time, when she corrects her children and supports their upbringing she is developing her empathy and coaching ability, and she is also delegating everything that can be delegated (especially physical matters), setting objectives and encouraging their achievement in the form of chores in the home, like setting the table, making the bed, taking out the rubbish or taking the dog for a walk, and constantly working in a team. If we want generations of good citizens and professionals capable of giving something more than an impeccable technical curriculum, we have to support the family and everything it involves as a place of education in the virtues of co-existence and character formation.

In the end, the family is this: a great team where everyone learns to share by developing the capacity to serve and do things for others, a habit which is very necessary in strengthening the bonds of any human organization, including the company. But for the family to continue to be a school of competencies for work and life, one must 'be there', one must 'make a family', share time together, and this is where the greatest shortfalls lie. It is a matter of organizing the home like a small company where everyone feels responsible for specific areas (job sharing) and also backs the whole; but for this it is essential to know how to include and involve the father and husband in the housework. On many occasions, it is the woman who takes on what has not been done, but this attitude acts as a damper on the development of the man and the family. Although it is true that she is the 'trump', of the household, it is not convenient to allow him to become to 'complacent'. By developing only one facet of his life, he would progressively acquire bad habits for the family and for the company. A professional like this, who abdicates his family facet, would end up working with the sole objective of efficiency without seeing the people behind. People who do not cultivate relations with those closest to them, the family, will find it difficult to do so in their work environment. This spiral would lead them to take more and more misguided decisions based on negative learning, with the source of action being impulsiveness. In this context, the company becomes more and more rigid, and the family (the eternal structure of flexibility and understanding) would surrender in the different cases... until it breaks up. It is here where women have an essential role in redirecting men towards the conciliation of work and family, helping them to become more whole, more human.

The development of skills in professional life also transfers to the family; the person can apply their competencies, habits and learning wherever they are, work or family. Amongst the professional competencies that have an influence in the household are time management, initiative, negotiation, teamwork, delegation, decision-making, stress management and people management.

The family, therefore, is no obstacle. Those interviewed recognized that family life balances the life of employees in general, including the focus they give their work, even though family obligations make them live with a permanent feeling of having a 'double working day' and not being able to do everything. These results are confirmed in studies as far apart in time as the one conducted by the University of Michigan in 1982[6] and the one carried out by the IESE in 2002.[7] The former concluded that the multiplicity of roles strengthens one's health and gives individuals security, resources and self-esteem, which has a direct effect on their professional competence. The greatest conflict is not generated by external factors; nor do policies or aid solve the problem (although they might contribute and alleviate), rather it is each person's way of reconciling work–family. Women with a double working day, despite feeling overloaded, do not confess to being more dissatisfied with their lives. Harmony is achieved thanks not so much to the convergence of external factors but to 'a particular way of dealing with the conflict', in other words, by using specific personal strategies that anticipate conflict and help to overcome it. It is a matter of mentally integrating both worlds, worlds which are not opposites at all, but which mutually complement each other and ask of each other.

A great deal of recent international research[8] shows us that the family is highly beneficial for our health. Married people have less likelihood than single people of suffering from a long-term illness or disability and have better survival rates in the event of any illness. A growing body of research also shows a link between the transcendent meaning of life and an improvement in physical health. Marriage is also associated with greater overall happiness, and children brought up by their own parents show better averages in terms of child mortality, health, schooling and fewer adolescent pregnancies.

Work–family conflicts: who is responsible?

> I have had in-depth training, I am not going to throw it all away... the children will come later.
>
> (doctor, 32)

> We want to get married but we have jobs in different cities.
>
> (manager, 34)

> Without my salary we could not pay our mortgage.
>
> (professional woman, 29)

Companies that are less compatible with families are those that have an obsessive working culture in which working many hours is a sign of dedication and therefore of professional promotion. Leaving work at the normal time is interpreted as a lack of commitment. This is the consequence of a reductionist view that involves a business system with a short-term, myopic view. The senior managers in the company also play an important role in this situation. If with their attitude, their working habits and their demands on subordinates they sustain this way of working, the culture of work addiction will be assured in the company. However, it is more advisable to 'treat' workaholics and not turn them into models for the others:

> The way the world is conceived, I do not think it is possible to have everything at the same time, a career and a family, 100 per cent. In my case, the most help has come from my mother, who has always made work compatible with family. I never have lunch at home because my work is very much tied up in customer relations and I like to spend as much time as I can with the people at work and exchange impressions. My mother is the one who goes to collect my daughter from school. I have no problem talking about work with my husband because I do not see work as a sacrifice, it is an activity that gives me much pleasure, much satisfaction. Do I work to live or live to work, I don't know what to say. To feel good in my family, I must feel good at work; that is basic.
>
> (market analyst, one daughter)

The worst thing were Mondays, we had board meetings and I got home at 10.30pm. I always found the lights out and the tray with dinner ready. I recognized that until that time, being a woman had always worked in my favour, but suddenly it turned me into somebody who was a problem.

(manager, two daughters)

The first necessary change is therefore socio-cultural. It involves reducing and reconciling timetables. One objective of governments, companies and individuals should be to draw closer to the European model, otherwise work will continue to absorb and cancel out the other facets of our life. Women's entry in the working world, very often adopting male roles and behaviour, makes this modern corporate 'dehumanization' even more obvious. We might blame women for the situation; however, we all know this is not true, but that we have turned the number of hours spent at work into the central value of companies and not the people who work there and their output capacity.

We live immersed in a life where we overvalue to an extreme degree paid work over other spheres of life. This concept translates into convictions such as: time is basically money; individual value is determined by work; 'my' self-realization is above everything; and the only ticket to success involves developing the male-style competitiveness and aggressiveness. According to the English consultant Austin Knight, 37 per cent of executives work more than 50 hours a week, and this number only increases with the importance of the management post they hold. According to the 1993 Community work directive, the maximum length of the working week in Europe may be 48 hours; however, all European countries have laws lowering this figure to 40 hours a week or even less. In recent years, several European countries have decided to reduce this to 40 hours a week in order to create employment. This is the case of Ireland (39), Germany (38), Belgium (38), Denmark (37), and especially France, where the working week is 35 hours. Outside the European Union, the United States and Japan have working weeks of 40 hours, with much higher figures in China (44) and India (48).

Spain is the country where the most hours are spent 'at work', which does not necessarily mean 'working'. Our working culture is marked by 'dead hours' in front of the computer, in hallways or in the office. Furthermore, our workday is split by a large two-hour break at lunchtime when professional agreements are reached over restaurant tables or simply when the pace of work is broken just to be taken up again in the afternoon without any clear limit on closing hours.

In other European countries and even in the United States, a closing time of 5, 6 or 7 o'clock in the evening is respected. In Spain, only 14 per cent of companies follow an explicit policy of 'lights out' at a reasonable time. Forty-two per cent of companies do not consider themselves to have a workaholic environment, but only 32 per cent claim that part of the company cultures involves respect for employees' families.[9]

The consequences of this situation are well known: sick leave due to stress (more frequent than women's maternity leave), depression, absenteeism, burn-out syndrome and work addiction. In the family, the times they are together are reduced: 'We hardly see each other during the week, we leave each other notes on the fridge...it is impossible for us to argue', is the usual complaint of couples who say they get home without any energy for any family life. 'I often wonder whether it would be better to take something before being with the children, because I get home irritated,' says a mother of three children who is the manager of a sales department. The children spend a lot of time alone or with their grandparents and babysitters: 'When I had my second child, I realized I had not enjoyed my first.'

What is more, this business environment of long workdays and work addiction is not only harmful for people and for their families, but in the long term it is also unproductive and not economically sound for companies. The growing globalization of markets with ever larger companies and a work system in which interfunctional teams are growing in importance is a symptom of change. Furthermore, as has already been said, greater value is now placed on creative work and there are fewer hierarchical levels; the future is speaking to us about flexibility and management by objectives.

Human resource departments are therefore seeking new ways to motivate and gain the loyalty of talented staff and recruit new professionals. Let us not forget that in the not-too-distant future, the overall drop in population will add to the scarcity of professionals with certain job backgrounds. 'This problem will become serious in Catalonia in 2006 and the rest of Spain in 2010', we are told by a prestigious professional who prefers to remain anonymous. 'The truth is that we have an excess of certain types of professionals and a shortage of others.' With things like this, it is obvious that one of the priority objectives of companies given this new scene will be to retain talent, and this is something that is already happening in certain sectors. It would therefore be necessary to consider the need to design a new form of in-kind payment; instead of a performance car it might be possible to offer employees a family vehicle, or instead of other more personal perquisites, employees might be offered assistance to pay for babysitters or nurseries, for example.

Free time, private and family life in harmony with professional life and a job where it is possible to participate in new projects capable of challenging one's capabilities and aspirations; this is the new professional roadmap for many young people. All of these motivations conceal a new concept of success, more invisible, more subjective, more permanent and also in the end more committed to the company. Power and money have been and are still recognizable and desirable parameters; however, surveys reveal that managers in general would exchange salary for free time. Maybe they have been close witnesses to professional promotions followed by painful personal ruptures and have decided that they do not want to be yet another statistic:[10]

> The best decision I have taken is to recognize that I am not a superwoman, that I can't do everything well and that the family is the most important thing for me. I have had to overcome terrible feelings of guilt and hide the reality that my child was sick at home or that I had any problem, in order not to jeopardize my position. It was as if my family was a handicap or as if the company saw it that way.
>
> (area manager, married, 38, three children)

After decades of a giddy race for success, men and women in our century are now at a moment of taking stock. They are not only reviewing the models, the trends and the habits of their professional and family lives to see what has failed or why they are not compatible. The professional, the executive and the manager of our times wants greater authenticity in his 'life trajectory' and aspires to a level of self-realization and satisfaction that is no longer paid for by bonuses or promotions.

To achieve these objectives we must be capable of breaking certain patterns[11] and bear in mind that the future of the company lies not only in providing a wider range of family-responsible policies that encompass a larger number of services, programmes and flexibility for employees, but that it is also necessary to establish synergies between family and professional life. For Lotte Bailyn, this is not a marginal problem, rather a new productive opportunity that requires changes in the organization. This researcher basically talks about three moulds or stereotypes that have to be broken: time, commitment and fairness. Time and productivity have traditionally been related directly and proportionally, but it is being seen that policies such as flexibility can be a powerful stimulus for increasing output...and very often in less time.

On the other hand, the idea of commitment is no longer synonymous with an agreement on timetables but something more: work in exchange for money. Thanks to the flexibility often combined with large degrees of personal autonomy and responsibility, professionals are capable of developing greater commitment to the company, something which is not measured by hours spent at work but by the results and the effort shown in moments of truth.

Finally, fairness or the idea of a fair salary has become a different concept. If salaries are based mainly on objectives, the professionals themselves are capable of evaluating their remuneration and therefore of adjusting their level of satisfaction to reality. This concept basically favours women, who are usually the ones who demand flexibility in exchange for productivity and objectives.

Table 4.1 illustrates some of the synergies between work and family when employees have the ability to maintain a balance between family and working life.

Table 4.1   Balance between family and professional life

Effects on the person	Effects on the company
Capacity to concentrate and plan	• Greater efficiency (lower error rate) • Greater efficacy (higher production/hour rate) *Greater development of one's own skills, abilities and habits:* • Steep learning curve • Motivation to suggest changes and innovate
Satisfaction – motivation	• Greater facility for teamwork *Greater development of the skills, knowledge and habits of the product recipient:* • Greater added value for products • Greater customer satisfaction
Commitment – loyalty	• Job satisfaction, with the resulting fall in legal costs, compensations and strikes • Fall in undesired rotation • Increase in the company's appeal

Source: N. Chinchilla and M. Las Heras: DPON-2, 'Work as a Builder of the Individual, Family and Society: Looking at the Past and Projecting the Future', IESE Publishing, 2002.

Talking with the stakeholders

In our studies we have seen that the major issues that arise when talking to people who experience a conflict in reconciling work and family are the following: the lack of time and rushing; the culture of long workdays; the inner division or the feeling of doing both things (work and family) badly; the family as a 'second course', that is, experiencing the conflict between work and family as something unexpected (first they plan a career, then they get married and later the conflict comes); the absence of reproaches to the spouse concerning the 'distribution of household chores'; the lack of time for co-existence, reduced almost always to the weekend or a short time at night; and the infrequency with which hobbies are shared (they prefer to surf on Internet and do sports alone).

It is generally seen that if it is necessary to reduce working time to reconcile the two domains, women are almost always those who choose to reduce their working weeks (81 per cent of contracts) or work part time. In 80 per cent of the cases, work invades family life, and in the remaining 20 per cent, family life overflows or has an impact on working life. Amongst managers, the priority role is being a professional over being a parent or spouse. Younger professionals do not usually eat at home, and when they have the opportunity to do so, they do so at their parents' home and not at their own. The decision to have the first child is agreed, but the ultimate decision lies with the woman. They do sports to combat stress.

The way in which each person handles conflict can bring us closer to defining certain types of families depending on the type of conciliation achieved, which is what we shall deal with in the following pages. In each case, the decision taken is described by including the most meaningful testimony. Our study of dual-income couples[12] gives testimony by both men and women. Although the conflict is greater among women, conciliation is a concern for both of them.

When it is decided to change habits: there is a serious determination to change one of life's patterns or professional habits, including working part time, trying to get home earlier in the evening and having lunch together from time to time.

CASE A: J.L. is a thirty-five-year-old sales manager. Eighty per cent of his subordinates are women. Having an eight-month-old daughter has led him to take the decision to go home for lunch 'to enjoy my daughter and re-energize'. His wife has shortened her workday. Today he returns home at 7 o'clock in the evening instead of 8.30 to 'be home at my daughter's bath time'.

This decision to change ways or habits is associated with greater personal and marital satisfaction and also respect for the conflict; both areas (work and family) are intensely yet calmly attended to. Moreover, a further feature of this case is a certain distribution of physical tasks, which is essentially a way of also assuming more generic, ephemeral responsibilities concerning the home and the family, 'I deal with the dishwasher, she puts on the washing machine and irons. The cleaning is done by the cleaning lady.'

Therefore, time together is sought, although there are also personal spaces: 'On Saturday mornings we go out for a walk and the three of us are together; in the afternoon I go off to play hockey.' There are fewer dinners with friends, not because of chronic tiredness caused by work, as is reflected in other interviews, but because there is a will to reserve an area for privacy, because they want to be with their daughter: 'On Saturdays I bath and feed her,' says J.L.

Although there have been hard moments or times in the company, this executive does not take work home because he believes that 'he already spends enough hours in the office and can deal with it there'.

Since he works in a fifty-person SME, he considers that the values are set in practice by personal style and the actions of those who are at the helm. He thinks that family and personal satisfaction influences the way problems are resolved. During the day he is 100 per cent available, but at weekends he turns off his mobile phone. This is a tacit agreement with the company.

'I have negotiated extensions of leave for breast-feeding for my female employees and I give the family priority because experience has shown me that if this works well, there are fewer problems at work.'

CASE B: M.S., thirty-one, consultant, married and mother of an eight-month-old daughter. In her testimony she ponders the decision of a female manager who is taking on her new situation by temporarily reducing her working hours. She is a Barcelona representative of an office with its headquarters in Madrid. She currently works part time and was able to choose this option after working very hard the previous year and having established in her company the bases of a work organization that has enabled her to reduce her working week. In short, she has taken advantage of a positive working climate and managed to delegate responsibilities after 2 o'clock in the afternoon. Her day goes like this: 'At 8.05 the babysitter comes. Juan and I leave home together and he drops me off at the underground. At 2.20 he picks me up from the underground and we go home. We now have lunch together every day; this wasn't the case before. We can also have a nap. The truth is that he is very happy. He comes home every day to see his daughter. In the afternoon I stay at home with Maria and do the ironing.'

She recognizes that sometimes it is tempting to accept other jobs, which goes against the decision they have taken. 'They offered me the chance to work in a speech pathology centre on Monday afternoons as an associate. I accepted, then I realized it was absurd. I had chosen part-time work to be with my daughter and I was bargaining off an afternoon with the added aggravation that my mother in-law had to come to do the ironing that day.' Might M.S. be fleeing ironing on Mondays, one of the most cumbersome tasks with the most short-lived results and one of the least-valued chores in the home? This same attitude, a flight from the home, or rather from the chores, is constantly reflected in the frequency with which many couples surveyed eat in their parents' home at lunchtime. It is curious to see the sacrifice of privacy in favour of comfort and saving, particularly taking into account that this custom, frequent during the working week, might jeopardize the needed space of autonomy for the new family.

In the evening, things are organized so that there is habitual, ongoing contact among the three of them. 'He usually arrives when I am bathing her and stops to watch. Then he gives her her bottle while I make dinner,' a typical scene of 'recovery' that can make up for many absences during the working day. These times are important for establishing relationships and increasing the family's overall satisfaction. Parents who arrive when their children have already gone to bed feel the conflict between work and family even more acutely.

M.S. and her husband have decided to get rid of the computer at home, a way of preventing work from invading their private life.

When everything remains the same: there is a determination not to change patterns or life habits. In such cases, instead of including rationality, time is allowed to go by, but time doesn't sort anything out and only makes matters worse. Decisions have to be taken.

J.T. is a businessman, married with three children (six, four and one and a half years of age). He has two courier companies. His wife works in a family business, which allows her to have a working day of 8 am to 3 pm. As she goes to work earlier, he drops the children off at school. He helps out but does not change his habits: he eats wherever he can. At the weekend he spends time keeping track of their bank accounts on the Internet, although he usually spends a little family time, he goes for a walk with the children. His plans include moving forward the time he leaves the office by one and a half hours in the evening to be able to spend more time at home, although he also says that 'more than getting home early, the secret lies in organizing your day well'. He gives more importance to quality time and mental time than to physical attention and physical time. Furthermore, he says that more than once he has gone home because he had reached his limits ('and if the company has to fail then let it fail'), as an occasional reaction, caused more by tiredness at work than by family demands.

In his case, work invades family life, not because he takes pending matters home, but because it takes up many more hours than his family. The secret why this situation does not actually cause a conflict lies in the fact that 'everything is fine at home, we do not argue and everything is going well'. The good marital relationship prevents them from facing up to the conflict, but the truth is that the conflict, though latent, is there.

When the children are a variable that directly affects the intensity of the conflict, and there is also work instability.

CASE A: J.P., an external consultant, and I.I. are the parents of two girls, six and three years old. She works in a Japanese company under fantastic conditions, and he is self-employed. The good marital harmony between them saves them from the underlying conflict. On several occasions throughout the interview, she said, 'I would like to reduce my working day, but J's work, although it is going well now, is not stable. I lose a lot if I reduce my salary.' Her office is five minutes from home and she has an hour and a quarter at lunch-time to see her daughters, but she has to return to work in the afternoon and this is what she finds difficult. She has the help of her in-laws as babysitters, who also resolve the problem of lunch at midday; however, she complains that she does not see her daughters very much and that there is not the same working climate as before (she moved to this branch of the company very recently). Her boss is an inflexible woman and this causes her a lot of stress. The facts once more confirm that the objective burden of work or family, rather the human relations established at work, are the determining cause of the stress. 'I do not usually take work home, I do not feel that work is overwhelming me or invading my family life; however, when I come home with worries or do not feel appreciated or feel they are taking me for granted, my daughters pay for my bad mood.' Although on eight days out of ten, her husband arrives home at 8 o'clock or 9 o'clock in the evening, she does not show a feeling of abandonment or lack of marital time together at all. 'We make up for it at the weekend. He then spends a lot of time with the girls, he goes with them to play sports and I do things at home more calmly.'

CASE B: O.G. is a businesswoman and the owner of a tax consultancy and F.H. is the director of a business school. They are parents of two children aged six and four. Over a period of six years she has experienced the entire process of setting up a company, becoming pregnant with her first child and the second and breaking up with her partner. She admits that she likes the independence of having her own business and that her husband has never reproached her in any way, not even for hypothetical mistakes. Furthermore, he also calls on her as an occasional speaker and teacher at his school.

As regards the family organization, once more it is the husband who deals with the early morning. 'He has breakfast with them. If he doesn't do this, he doesn't see them...' He is also the one who takes them to school. 'I have negotiated with my company to be able to go to work at 10 o'clock in the morning, in this way I see them for a time and I relieve my wife a little.' At weekends he helps them with their homework and each day usually calls about 7 o'clock in the evening to talk to them on the phone. As a negative habit, 'We stay up at night, and the next day it's impossible to wake us up and it's not because of the children but because sometimes we take work home to do at night.'

The only measure she adopts to reduce the conflict she feels between work and family is to get off work at half past four to collect the children from school and take them home. She stays with them for half an hour and returns to the office until 8 o'clock. Her dilemma often comes down to choosing whether to be alone with her husband, who usually arrives at half past eight, or also sharing weekend plans with the children. 'I don't see either him or them. We love classical music and going to the opera. Two weekends ago we wanted to go without the children, but in the end we included them. I have the feeling that during the weekend I have not been with them much, and this upsets me a lot.'

Although she has had no problems granting shorter workdays to young mothers in her company, she only took three weeks of maternity leave. She prefers to work with women because they are better in terms of organization, and she believes they are more productive. However, she does complain that when there is a lot of work, people do not rise to the occasion and in the end it is her family that suffers.

She detects an underlying conflict with respect to the sharing of household chores. 'If one of the children has to be collected because he is ill, it is always me who goes. When my husband tells me that he is tired, I feel like saying "you might be tired, but I had to leave work to collect the children".' Sometimes the conflict arises between dealing with a customer or a child, and this is terrible for her: 'Although you are professional, you have to play a role in your family that nobody can fill.'

As a positive aspect of motherhood, she highlights that in her case it has helped her to prioritize and above all to 'separate' areas. 'Before, I would take a problem home from work and turn it over and over; now this is impossible and I turn off when I leave.' With respect to values, she identifies fully with the personal values that she tries to transfer to her company. 'My company is like a family,' she says. This idea is also shared by her husband.

Though always on the verge of stress and with a permanent feeling of not covering everything, this woman places enormous value on motherhood: 'I think there should be a suitable framework of freedom so that everyone might reconcile the two in their own way. Maternity leave should be one year. What's more, when I am asked what the ideal time is to have a child I always say do it now or you will never do it.'

No children . . . more time together, but . . . there is the Internet! In these cases, at least theoretically, there was more time for both of them, more time to spend together. However, the interviews revealed that it is these couples who spend the most time working. In fact, since the family facet does not exist, these people become work addicts because the only thing that identifies them is their profession.

CASE A: We find almost idyllic cases, such as M.M., a twenty-eight-year-old teacher, married for eight months to E.V., a financial adviser, and still living out their honeymoon. 'In the morning, he makes the beds and takes the plates out of the dishwasher. If I get home late one day, he does everything necessary, like dinner. What's more, every time one of us does something good at home, the other congratulates them with a kiss.' In the morning, they have breakfast together, and although they do not have lunch together, at half past seven in the evening, many days they are both already home. At lunchtime, he has lunch in his parents' house and she has lunch at the school where she works. Neither of them brings work home, although he does spend some time on the Internet if he has to prepare a proposal for a customer. They talk about work without it conflicting with their private life. He is very absorbed by work, especially mentally: 'you never turn off,' he says. At weekends they usually go out, they often go to the mountains together.

With respect to the subject of having a child, she says that she is frightened 'that he will leave her alone with everything', and she is also worried about 'being overwhelmed with children at work and children at home'. Nevertheless, at another point in the interview she says, 'I do not have any career plans, I just want to be happy like now. If I have to be in the same place as I am now, then that is perfect. If I get bored and need a change, I hope to be able to find one. I am not looking for promotion or for rises or anything, I just want to be happy with what I do at work and that this complements and helps me to be happy in my personal life. Plans, very few. In terms of a family, to have children, children, children, as many as I can, because I love them. Maybe I'm saying this now because I haven't got any, but whatever. The truth is I love children, it is what I love most.'

CASE B: A situation somewhat more extreme is the case of C.L., a public relations officer in a German multinational, and F.G., a division manager of pharmaceutical laboratory, both thirty-one years old and both with a master's degree in business management. They have been married for two years and do not have any children because, according to her, they should be more mature and have a slower pace at work. Both work an average of 10 hours a day. She has lunch every day at her parents' house and they usually take advantage of Sunday afternoons to prepare the things that are pending for the following day; in other words, both suffer from a conscious, ongoing invasion of their private life by work, not only during the week but also at the weekends. On top of all this, she has to travel frequently to trade fairs, spending a week away from home.

Both she and her boss, being management personnel, have a contract outside the collective agreement; that is, 'the company has its established timetables, but we are not included'. The result of this is that meetings are last thing in the evening, as established by her boss. 'If you have to deal with anything with him, you cannot go home.'

She feels the situation should change; there are no policies in her company to favour reconciling work and family life, but 40 per cent of the personnel in the marketing area are women. 'Women are a talent that has to be retained,' she says. 'And nowadays they are better prepared than men. I am in favour of everyone designing their own timetable; many things can be done at home and with great productivity.' She complains that she sleeps badly and shows a certain fear of becoming pregnant due to the reprisals that her boss might take.

As a means of combating stress, she goes to the gymnasium with her husband, and to do this they get up three-quarters of an hour earlier in the morning. He is reserved, he does not talk about work with her and also sleeps badly. 'I wake up thinking of things, and when I take a long time to go to sleep it is because I am turning something over in my head from work.' On the other hand, he recognizes that 'most of the time we are so tired that we hardly talk to each other'. Another conflict can also be seen, in this case between the values of the company and personal values. 'In the company, I have to be colder than I would like,' he says.

CASE C: When both partners (telecommunications engineers) work in the same company and also in such a competitive sector as IT, things become more complicated. This is the case of M.B., a senior IT consultant, and J.D., a support engineer. They are both now twenty-seven and decided that they should at least be in different departments. He explains, 'Although we go down to have a coffee from time to time to see each other . . . we talk more about work than other couples. I don't know if this is good or bad; it sometimes seems to me that we talk too much and I think that if the company went under or there were readjustments, we would both end up in the street.' This attitude or feeling of instability in both professionals is surprising because they both have permanent posts. 'We work in a company where your PC and a mobile phone are everything you need. You do not have a fixed post in the office, the posts are virtual.' Although they have almost two hours for lunch, they do not usually eat together, maybe because they do not physically coincide in the office. 'You're never sitting in the same place or doing the same job. Some days you eat at 1 o'clock and others at three.'

He is not usually physically in the office more than one or two days a week, and the rest of the time he is working with customers. 'One agreement among colleagues is that mobile phones are never turned off . . . in return, if one day you finish at 5 o'clock you go home, but this doesn't happen very often. She has more pressure. Her projects have a deadline, but I can kind of let work build up and then do it within the deadlines that I set.' They recognize that during the week they usually do the housework, chat or stroll in the evening, while on Sundays they tend to work for an average three hours each at home, she more than he does. There are also mutual complaints at the time they get home, 'Most times when we talk about work it is about the timetables, the other's long working hours or the problems derived from the working environment, never the work itself.' However, both agree that they are at an age when they have to show the company their value, without entering into whether what they put in is fair or not.

As regards the possibility of her giving up work for a time to care for children, J.D. is the only one of the men interviewed who says that he is in favour, as long as she agrees. He believes that the work–family conflict is a subject that must be resolved in the personal sphere, but that to do so there must be a suitable framework of freedom and flexibility. She says that spending two or three nights a week away from home, depending on the projects, makes her feel the conflict more acutely. 'The most I do is save one night, but no more. Today these projects are mine. If I said no to going to Madrid, I wouldn't be either flexible or virtual, it could mean something more in my working situation, for sure.'

At other times she says it is impossible for her 'to separate work from my private life, the stress goes with me'. In both cases, time is scarce: 'Newly weds need lots of time to be together.' 'Is it so terrible if they don't have it?' 'Well, it's not so terrible but you obviously don't develop the way you should as a person.'

A trick called . . . 'my company'. The business pattern is adopted: the company's interests are placed before personal or family interests. There is a lack of rationality and strength to recognize what is happening. This is a clear case of self-deception and justification.

It can and in fact does happen that an economist with an MBA and the mother of a daughter might so identify with the interests of the company that they can begin to think that the problem of the work–family conflict not only lies with them, but that if it is not resolved, they are also responsible. She enters a company on an internship with a temporary contract. When they find out that she is pregnant they do not renew the contract. She has the baby, but without taking maternity leave. After six months she comes back to the same company and works full time to show her worth. She is frightened of asking for a reduced workday and does so only after a year and a half; she does not want to cause a problem for the company. When her daughter falls ill, the conflict reaches its worst point, however, she holds on until she has completed the project she is currently on. At the same time she recognizes that she does not like to be at home: 'when my daughter was born, the walls closed in on me'. Her husband 'did not want to hear about her giving up work, not even temporarily'.

Furthermore, she says that having a child and reducing her workday has slowed up her career. 'You don't do such interesting things, they don't give you large projects,' although once more a twist of business appears in the situations (reduced workday due to maternity) to its own benefit; 'I am going to replace one of the bosses, although

I am not formally going to be a boss. I am going to do the work, but they are not going to promote me.'

What is striking, however, is the actual use of the reduced work-day: 'I get up at 8 o'clock. Two months ago, I got up at seven but now it is eight, because my daughter sleeps longer. My daughter is our alarm clock. I have a shower, have breakfast, and leave her clothes ready. At half past eight, Maria arrives to change her and take her to the nursery. I go to work between half past eight and 9 o'clock. I used to go to work by motorcycle and took ten minutes to get there, now I go by bus and it takes half an hour. I work from 9 o'clock to 2 o'clock or half past two and go to my parents' house for lunch, because my daughter eats in the nursery; she goes there from 9 o'clock to 5 o'clock, is very happy and I am very pleased. She used to go home for lunch, Maria would pick her up, give her lunch and put her to bed. When I came home for lunch I found her asleep. When I was working full time I used to go to work, I had lunch at 2 o'clock and my daughter was asleep. At 3 o'clock, I would go to work again and not get home until 8 o'clock. There were days when I didn't even see her awake. When I had a shorter working day, when my daughter only went in the mornings, I would get home and she was asleep, but I stayed home and spent afternoon with her. Now she stays in a nursery until five, I go and pick her up at 4.45pm and have a chance to have a family life. I usually get home between 7 o'clock and 8 o'clock and my husband gets home between nine and ten because he does sports, not because he is working.' In fact, she actually gets home at the same time as before and also has lunch in her parents' house, and her daughter does not see her until 5 o'clock in the afternoon. In this case there is an impression that the shorter workday is more to rest from her intense years working rather than to reconcile work and family, a fine example of the consequences of overloading. At the weekend, she finds time to go out with friends while he does sports, and when they go out it is to do the shopping or on errands, and they do so separately 'because it is quicker if you don't go with the child'.

With respect to the company, she does not believe that it has values that serve her personally or that she could adopt; in fact, she has decided to ignore the situation by adopting a conformist attitude. At the same time, she has a clear feeling of guilt: 'Alright, I am a boss and I understand that what I am doing is not fair on my boss. If I feel sorry for anyone, it's for my boss, because I appreciate him a lot. I am aware that what I'm doing is not fair. He would find it more comfortable to have a full-time person for anything he might need; if you have a team, I am a drawback. Although I work well, he would prefer to have me on the project that he had assigned for me. If he has to choose between me and a guy, well it's obvious, but the fact that I am now asking for a shorter timetable does not mean that in five or six years' time I cannot work harder again. The thing is that since the philosophy is that at forty you have either reached a certain position or you are worthless, that's terrible because now I am thirty and when my children are six or seven I will start to work harder again, 100 per cent, but I will be too late for the company.' She seems to have a clear view of her professional career as something constantly rising (the traditional view of the male world), without considering that it is better to think of trajectories, with professional plateaux that may seem like a loss in one sense, but in another are enormous wealth for one and all.

Her dilemma lasts right to the end: 'I understand the company, the company is looking for profits, the company is not interested in having women. Either the government establishes a series of rules that help companies to have women that can combine work and family, or things will not work out.'

In all of these cases (illustrating the integration of working and family life), the importance of individual or family decisions is obvious. To truly be an agent of change, a woman must take an active stance. Even in the most staid companies, it is possible to ask for surprising margins of autonomy if you know how to negotiate and if a woman anticipates the problems by proposing possible solutions.

5
Family-responsible Companies

'We have reached a situation where parents are employed, but the labour market does not take into account the fact that people have family responsibilities. We tend to base employment on the rules of a continuous worker working full-time, and this causes some problems for men and many problems for women.'

Peter Moss

'It is the company (stronger) and not the family (weaker) that should notice the natural, beneficial connection between the working life of a person and all of the other relevant aspects of their life.'

Carlos Llano

Today more than ever there is a strong relationship between the presence of a family-responsible culture and the effective development of a company. It involves regarding an employee as something more than an individual subject that expects to be rewarded with salary and training. These policies bear in mind the new profile of their staff, men and women, for whom the system of priorities has changed and the family occupies an important place. Personal private life is a further variant of the concept of quality of life and the magic word is 'balance'. If this is achieved, as has already been said, the company will benefit: higher productivity for the time worked, loyalty, retention of the best talent and creation branding the job market.[1]

Companies are more and more aware that a personal balance affects output and productivity. Moreover, technical competencies are not enough to satisfactorily cover a job, as most of the competencies needed to be able to contribute to achieving the business objectives lie in the area of emotional intelligence. We need open, creative minds capable of handling the obstacles with sportsmanship. This gives rise to new forms of assessment and compensation which range from training to flexibility and support for one's life trajectory. All of this makes up the business policies of family-responsible companies, which deserve a more in-depth analysis.

There are three main factors behind the adoption of specific measures: the type of work a specific worker does, the economic development of the country and the level of working stability. A fourth factor should also be added here: the point in an individual's professional career, an aspect which is highly related to the career design that has been planned by the individual and the company itself. The United States is the country where we find greatest development in programmes designed to reconcile family and working life, and the multinationals are the leaders in this area. Very often it is the headquarters that prods its Spanish subsidiaries into action by arguing that they are ten years behind in these kinds of policies.

In any case, the initiatives taken from the company only complement many other measures taken by the different social stakeholders, including the state and the public administrations, as we have seen in the second chapter and which, summing up, come down to legislation on motherhood/fatherhood and specific measures aimed at conciliation, direct aid for the family and economic subsidies for the number of children, indirect aid or tax breaks, infrastructure and labour reforms to facilitate conciliation.

Pro-family values, programmes and policies

The company can adopt policies, programmes, be responsible for the family . . . but it is unable to protect workers from themselves.

(account executive)

When a man works more time it is viewed that he does so in favour of his family; if a woman does this, we think that she is putting her family aside.

(human resources manager)

I have decided that the question that is worth asking is not what job I want to have, but what life I want to lead.

(stock market analyst, separated)

Our IFREI study (IESE Family Responsible Employer Index)[2] carried out amongst Spanish companies in 1999, 2001 and 2003 is the first step on the way to what is already seen as a series of work and social changes and a new source of compensation for employees that management will have to learn to evaluate and promote as much as salary. We have selected the results of the IFREI 2001, published in 2002, as being paradigmatic of the situation, although throughout the study we refer to the trends noted in the past four years.

More than 2,000 surveys sent to human resource managers and employees in the largest companies in Spain and more than twenty personal in-depth interviews were the starting point. The first time, only 150 companies replied, that is, 7 per cent of the total, a percentage which in some way constitutes a criterion of self-selection.

The main factors behind change, when changes occurred, were the presence of women at all levels of the company, personal involvement of the board of directors in encouraging policies and cultural change, and change in social awareness of the subject.

Family-responsible companies are those where the business strategies and intrategies (policies that pursue employee involvement and commitment) consider the employee's family as yet another stakeholder[3] in the company. In fact, there are already companies that put this forward as an argument to attract and retain the most talented staff in a job market where there are good technical CVs but a lack of mature people with a capacity for commitment.

Most companies that decide to gather data on this subject do so by means of an annual or biannual questionnaire concerning employee satisfaction. The responsibility for work–family concerns is often formally assigned to an employee, or sessions are organized to sensitize and train managers and mid-level managers to deal with such matters.

The fact is that in the year 2002, only 7 per cent of Spanish companies surveyed with more than 100 employees had a programme of family-responsible policies designed and implemented. If we take into account companies that are currently establishing or studying the possibility of setting up a programme to harmonize work and family, this figure rises to 30 per cent. The low percentage may be explained in the light of claims such as those put forth by certain managers: 'It costs money...' or 'But are there really so many measures that can be implemented?' It has even been claimed that: 'Our payment policy is sufficient,' 'This subject belongs in the realm of public policy, not the company.'

Generally speaking, the corporate culture of a company, that is, the series of corporate values that inspire it, is the determining factor for there to truly be harmony between work and family in the life of each employee.

It is a fact, frequently seen, that formal policies are not sufficient to create a family-compatible environment, and that for one to be fully implemented the support of the corporate culture is needed, often in a more informal way, not necessarily written down in a document, but which constitutes the climate, the atmosphere breathed in the company on a certain matter, in this case the attitude towards employees' families. Therefore, the managers' attitude and more specifically their explicit and implicit stances is essential. In this sense the managers are once again key players, since they are the mirror of the whole company, as are mid-level managers, since they are the ones who decide on a daily basis whether or not the policies that facilitate conciliation are implemented.

In theory, as has already been said, the multinationals, encouraged by their headquarters abroad, where such policies had long been in place, were the first to implement this kind of programme in Spain. 'The size makes it possible to cover the cost of these services,' some say. However, there are many measures that do not require significant investment, maybe just a change in habits (timetable, workplace).

The personal values and the managers' own training determine the way and degree to which they approach these policies within the company. On a secondary level, but no less important, is the tolerance of the rest of the colleagues when they have to take on a greater workload from their colleagues in the event of emergencies and unplanned absences.

Today, the leading programmes in companies are still those on equal opportunities, followed by those on diversity. The programmes aimed at reconciling work and family increased considerably in the year 2003 and will continue to do so in the coming years, because the flaw is there, and there is a true need to alleviate it desired by one and all and at the same time a widespread demand from Spanish society.

However, fostering this situation requires a change of mentality, overcoming it by rising above it: it is not just a question of *reconciling* but also *integrating* work and family in neutral harmony. The awareness-raising stage has already been undertaken in many areas; now many companies and public administration bodies are going into action.

The measures, one by one: case studies and solutions

The different family-responsible business policies may be grouped into four areas.

The first group deals with *flexibility in time and space*. The former is, in fact, the most coveted package of measures and also, we believe, the one that involves the least cost. It is sufficient to have a good incentive policy (flexibility itself is an incentive) and make it clear that there is management by objectives and not by controlling the time the staff is present. The argument is a simple one: both work and the family require time and energy. These needs do not follow a strict timetable of a certain number of hours a day, between certain times, so many days a week. Both the requirements of work and those of the family tend to fluctuate depending on what each one requires at each moment: more or less intense seasons, life cycles, stages in one's career and unexpected events:

> Overall, I see two different problems: the working environments hostile for mothers, and women who put off having a family and miss the boat. Therefore, I believe that a company that wants to have women must design alternative work posts, such as shared posts. It must also design the work posts and think of the people that can fill them in line with the people leaving. At school, we combine a half-day by a teacher close to retirement with a half-day by another with many children who must slow down her career for several years. We reconcile the good of the company with the good of people, and this does not cause problems by comparison, because we do it with all the people we can. This afternoon, I suggested a year's leave to a person who is pregnant and does not feel well. In this case, she is able to accept it, but there are family economies that cannot. In this way, when people come back, they do so with very good working pace and great creativity.

During the maternity leave, the teacher is still linked to a substitute teacher, which makes it easier for her to return and continue. There is no problem for those that take a year off, because each year the pupils are different. I recognize that in an educational environment there is a special sensitivity to caring for people, which is why these policies are better developed.

(school headmistress, married, 42, five children)

In some sectors and jobs, time and physical presence are no longer relevant criteria for assessment and pay; instead objectives and results are. Therefore, strict timetables and controls on the number of hours worked are replaced by flexible timetables, self-control and assessment based on objectives. In all of these a very important role is played by the control the professionals themselves have over their work, so that there are no overflows from one domain to another (from work to family or the family possibly invading the professional realm):

We have half an hour's flexibility on coming in and when we leave, too. Each bank branch organizes itself. There are no part-time contracts, but there are one-third, one-quarter or half-time reductions for mothers who have to look after sick children. Of course they can and must ask for it if necessary. For our part, we only take the precaution of checking with the unit head. Today there are several hundred people who have turned to this measure.

(savings bank where 47 per cent of the staff are women)

The range is very broad; one can talk both of short absences from work (half an hour) and long absences (one year), depending on the systematic or temporary needs of the family: absence due to family emergency, flexibility in days' leave, free time for training, leave to look after young children and leave to look after the sick or disabled, a shorter workday, flexible timetables and part-time work:

Mothers have first dibs when choosing their leave and flexible timetables. Of the two employees at the call centre, the one who is a mother of two has preference when choosing holiday times and in choosing a shift in the morning compatible with caring for her children... We always cover leaves and sickness with external staff in order not to overload the personnel.

(computer SME, fifty employees)

According to OECD data from the year 2002, part-time work in Spain accounts for 8 per cent of employment, twice the figure of the previous year. The increase of part-time work and reduced timetables in Spain is due to the greater participation of women in the working world, not due to the fact that the conditions of this kind of contract have improved in our country. In Europe, one-third of all women turn to this formula, whereas only 6.2 per cent of men do so. This means that it is something that is on the rise but still rarely implemented if we compare it with Holland, where 40 per cent of the employed population works part time.

If we look at it from the standpoint of children's needs, the results are interesting. Studies such as the one by professors John Ermichs and Marco Francesconi of the University of Essex indicate that the school failure rate is much lower when mothers work part time. These children also have a lower risk of psychological problems when they are adults. Therefore, the policy-makers must nurture shorter working days for at least one of the parents. However, the task of changing the attitudes towards the relative value of work and being parents may be difficult, as large companies tend to consider higher levels of responsibility at work as something irreconcilable with a high degree of family commitment. This approach is also based on the belief that time spent at the workplace is equivalent to commitment and output. Changing this mentality would involve tightening the screw once more on joint family responsibility: men must assume more responsibility with their children. Ultimately, this entails viewing the subject not only in economic terms: 'People say that we cannot accept policies such as the extension of maternity leave, but maybe as a society we cannot accept not having them.'[4]

Furthermore, the worker adopting a part-time workday at a certain time does not necessarily mean that they have to miss the career boat:

> I have two children, aged three and five, and am finally reconciling my work and family life. For me it is important to feminize the work environment, to contribute long-term values, to demonstrate that it is possible, good and necessary to take the reins of all aspects of my life, and that this also positively affects my company. I 'risked' asking for a reduction in my workday, and now I am in an internal communication post that seems tailor-made for me. I believe that I bring the values I adopt in my personal life into

my company and enrich it. I think that it is necessary to avoid a cookie-cutter staff profile in companies, it is not only the 'high potential' young workers who sustain the company. Sometimes a good dose of common sense demonstrated in daily life can mean the difference between success and failure in a work project. One's career is long, and I believe that in the case of women it is much more fruitful after the early years of motherhood. At least I believe I'm getting the best of it, and I am wiser, more competent, more committed. With a reduced working day, I give my company much more and for much less time than before. What for others might seem like a step backwards for me has entailed 'sustainable development' as a person.

(expert in environmental applications, two children)

In many sectors and fields (consultancy, sales), flexibility in the times people go to work and leave facilitates the sharing of chores between the couple (taking the children to school, doctors, shopping). With respect to the economy, the spread of this formula goes hand-in-hand with a rise in the service sector: trade, technical services, real estate and hostelry.

Although two-thirds of companies guarantee workers their posts after an extended leave, only one-third of them have an employee replacement policy. This means that two-thirds do not take it and that the work falls upon their colleagues. In this way, the only thing that is achieved is that leave-taking comes to be frowned upon. The extension of maternity leave beyond what is stipulated by law is the measure most highly valued by women, followed by care of sick children, parents and disabled relatives. Less deep-rooted in Spain are paid free time, sabbaticals, rest periods or professional plateaux and the unpaid holidays so characteristic of other cultures.

It was recently made known on the Internet[5] that the Australian subsidiary of the pharmaceutical company Aventis had offered employees returning from maternity leave more than 6,000 Australian dollars (3,585 American dollars) for caring for their children. This incentive was brought in as an attempt to retain their female workers after discovering that half of the women who ask for maternity leave do not return.[6] Other institutions offering paid leave include the Catholic University of Australia, which gives 52 weeks of paid leave (12 weeks on full pay and the rest on 60 per cent). *Flexibility in space* refers to the workplace. It involves providing the option of working at home or in the office. Employees then have greater control over their timetable and workspace. Some policies of this kind are telecommuting (thanks to the use of laptop computers and Internet connections by the company) and the use of video conferences, which avoids more trips from one town to another or even between countries, than are strictly necessary:

> Here 80 per cent of the personnel have laptop computers and the other 20 per cent do not wish work to invade their private life, and we respect this. Our programmes for harmonizing work and family life are audited by an outside company, because we want everything to be truly useful. We regard the cost of all this, if this can be said, to be marginal because we have found that there is a clear benefit, which is the satisfaction of our employees and therefore an increase in their output.
>
> (multinational in the IT sector)

The ethical aspect of these measures could be mentioned with respect to the suspicion that their use could be a subterfuge of the company as an ante-room for not only a spatial breakaway, but also for dismissing workers. Although it is necessary to bear in mind this possibility, we must not lose sight of the example of countries such as Switzerland and Holland, where employees do not lose their value and are not diverted from their careers by the number of hours they work or their physical workplace, and a sign of this is the varied grids of staff work planning in companies in these countries:

> We have a manager who uses this option and also has a reduced timetable (six hours); however, a person who has been in the company for under a year asked to be able to work from home but was not allowed. We believe that it is necessary to know them better before giving them this vote of confidence.
>
> (SME with fifty employees)

For some people at certain stages of their life, flexibility policies prevent them from being rotated or permanently leaving the job market, since they can choose to become self-employed or to set up their own company, if caring for dependents (parents, children) or other personal reasons lead them to do so.

The boy has cerebral paralysis. His mother worked in a company where flexibility was practically zero. The father was an employee of ours. We offered to install an ADSL line for him and allow him to work with a laptop computer from home until 5 o'clock in the afternoon.

(service sector company)

A second area of family-responsible business policies concerns *social benefits/salary perks*, which are also widely implemented in Spanish companies. This entails medical insurance for employees and their families, pension plans, life insurance, restaurant tickets, etc. and other aid that can help the family get by or at least give them a certain ease of mind in difficult times.

At a well-known company, the employees have a pension plan in which the company contributes twice what the employees put in. Furthermore, this company has corporate values which sometimes lead them to take measures 'beyond those of the law or the collective agreement'. This is demonstrated by the case of an anorexic employee that the company went to collect by ambulance from Galicia; or the temporary worker diagnosed with cancer that the company decided to give a permanent contract so that they would thus be assured their full health coverage; also the case of a worker with a quadriplegic father for whose flat the company paid to be adapted.

With respect to family medical insurance, there are companies that offer a dental plan for the whole family which covers a fixed amount per year. In some financial entities, a measure that fosters family solidity is the advantageous system of pension funds for their employees, and also the system of risk provision. Particularly appreciated, too, are risk coverage policies that cover contingencies of widowhood, orphanhood, absolute permanent incapacity and severe disability. Therefore, for example, if an employee should die, their widow or widower would receive 50 per cent of the deceased person's fixed annual salary and each of their children under 23 would receive 25 per cent of this salary, up to 125 per cent of the whole salary.

A well-known human resource manager indicates that this kind of help for families is less visible than a nursery, but that its value is far greater, 'For me, this is the maximum contribution to the conciliation of personal and working life. The greatest that exists and can exist. All of the others are anecdotal, shots in the dark, paternalism or for show.' In his opinion, work/family programmes often disguise protectionism. In short, it is necessary to treat employees as the adults they are. This means paying them well so that they might pay for the nursery and childcare services. It also involves offering generous benefits so employees might work without worry.

Other forms are disability insurance, Christmas bonuses, bonuses for marriage and the birth of children, as well as gifts from the company and trips as incentives for achieving objectives.

We have compiled the third area of policies under the name of *professional support*. This category consists of giving employees advice and training to balance work and family, to adapt the job to the new needs and to prepare the employee with specific training. It is also a question of extending their future employability:

> Our training centre receives 7,600 people each year. We have just brought in teaching English through the e-learning system for all employees.
>
> (multinational in the food sector)

Some examples include advice to expatriates, legal and financial advice, psychological and career support, etc. In all such cases, the family situation is explicitly taken into account:

> Our workplace health programmes cover such varied subjects as the prevention of breast cancer and osteoporosis. There is also therapy for stopping smoking, an activity that is prohibited throughout the building.
>
> (electricity company)

Whereas training in *time management* is a fairly frequent phenomenon (50 per cent of companies have done this at some time), what is surprising is the low percentage of companies (only 30 per cent) which offer courses on stress management for their employees, particularly when stress, as we have said, is one of the most important causes of work–family conflicts and work absenteeism:

> There are stress management courses as a way of reducing the pressure and the nature of bank work: customers have little time,

are demanding and require very fast transactions, and this takes its toll. Since these circumstances cannot change, we hope to increase the employees' level of self-control, as we regard this as a matter that is fundamental within the model of management by competencies and different from the training requirements of teamwork. But we also think of families. Stress is the worst conse-quence that they can suffer, in addition to a lack of time, and we hope to remedy it with courses such as these.

(financial services company)

Probably the reason why so few companies organize seminars on stress is the lack of true awareness of its importance: irritability, lack of concentration, absenteeism, aggressive behaviour, alcohol abuse and interpersonal conflicts are just a few of its consequences. Just as companies took decades to become environmentally responsible and prevent pollution, the same thing might happen now on becoming family responsible and avoiding work stress. If they do not do it for the health of their employees, they should do it for their own interests, as hundreds of studies have shown that stress reduces productivity.

What is also striking is the scant effort to implement programmes to support employees in their role as parents, bearing in mind that this is one of the subjects that most concerns young couples.[7] Training as parents and marital communication may be an interesting type of training for companies to provide.

In general, although most companies say that they do not force their employees to rise or leave when the promotion involves issues such as geographical mobility, so necessary in multinationals, almost half of those surveyed recognize that they accept that this transfer is a condition for promotion. This is the 'up or out' culture so frequent in the world of consultancy:

Last year we had a project in Athens. It required seventy people and lasted the whole year. We presented things very clearly, because we did not want to deceive anyone. We gave incentives for this mobility and distance with economic compensation, but we did not exert any pressure, and still less imposed penalties. However, what we all know is that rejecting an offer like that can limit your international career. In the case of a thirty-five-year-old with two young children who rejects such an offer, we would understand him not jumping at the opportunity and we would support him if he did. Maybe in the future another similar opportunity will arise ... or not. In this case, each person is responsible for his or her own actions.

(United States multinational)

Two-thirds of companies accept the existence of professional plateaux in their employees' careers, but only one-third admit to offering personalized help for people to consider this career. The problem becomes more acute in the case of professionals who have recently become mothers or marriages facing the dilemma of separation due to the company's demands for geographical mobility:

Given the nature of the company, people are often sent to different countries in the world for a period of time ranging from one to five months to work in customer companies. When assigning these destinations, these posts are never offered to parents, but rather to men or women who are married without children, because they usually accept them and have fewer problems combining stays with their spouses.

(SME with fifty employees)

Personal professional advice may be given by specialists (psychologists, doctors, lawyers), as happens in the case of the Employee Assistance Programmes already widespread in the United States and the United Kingdom. All Spanish companies have related internal or external medical service, but very few offer specialized advice. Doctors are not prepared to deal with the psychological, social, legal or financial problems that are frequently the true cause of absenteeism.

A fourth group of measures is known as *service policies* and includes different types of support that reduce the employee's load outside the company. The reasoning is not only that 'the smaller the workload outside the company, the less concerned they will be and the more they will work', but also that it acts to supplement the salary policy. People do not only need money to live but a greater quality of life: time and therefore services. Some examples are childcare, care for the elderly and household work such as cleaning, shopping, restaurant tickets, car parks, sports centres, information on nurseries or economic compensation for babysitters who have to cover the time they are absent at work:

Through our Internet portal, we offer a multitude of services organized around three concepts: community (including everything related to people and their families and information on nurseries and schools), training and professional. Thanks to the broad negotiation base coming from having a payroll of more than 12,000 employees, we managed to achieve valuable discounts on nurseries, gymnasiums and travel agencies.

(financial entity)

Most of these measures have a minimal cost for the company and a major effect on conciliation. It is only necessary to bear in mind that the company offers support in resolving different problems, but does not give a sole solution, thus leaving two things ensured: the right to a private life and therefore to all information about it, and parents' right to raise their children as they see most fit. This latter point is guaranteed in the most common options offered by companies: the school cheque and the nursery cheque to facilitate choice:

We give a €75 subsidy on the purchase of safety seats for babies.

(financial entity)

We pay for our employees' children's nursery.

(gas company, hydroelectric company,
company in the food sector)

We reserve places in nearby schools and have agreements with nearby nurseries.

(savings bank)

We subsidize certain expenses concerning our employees' children's education.

(pharmaceutical company)

We help to pay for holiday expenses and language stays for our employees' children.

(public company)

The order of importance, depending on the use made of these services in Spanish companies, is as follows: life insurance, retirement plan and restaurant tickets. These kinds of incentives, already traditional in our country, are now taking on new value. There are also specialized companies that handle these services externally, effectively and at a lower cost than if the company itself were to manage them.[8]

Towards a family-responsible company (FRC)

Obviously, any company that intends to lead their sector in the 21st century as an organization in search of benefit, providing society with a service and satisfying market demands, must take on a new factor: satisfying its employees not only through payment policies but also through career plans and support for the conciliation of their family and professional life. The trend is unstoppable and supported by the proposal, as a new requirement, set out in the new version of ISO 900.

Some companies, such as those that take part in the +Family plan developed by the Spanish Federation of Large Families, have already been made aware of this and have decided to include advantages and specific projects in their business lines which entail social recognition for the work of families with a larger number of children.

The objective is for companies to take on their share of social responsibility when protecting and supporting the family as a key element for development and economic and social welfare, and for them to foster effective conciliation between work and family life. We are undoubtedly at the most interesting point of reflection; that of the construction of business culture and nurturing of a public opinion that is favourable and proactive in this area.

It has taken us many years to understand and assimilate the many benefits brought about by the concept of environmental ecology as a form of responsible exploitation of the scarce natural resources of our planet, based on respect for nature; to understand that we are 'temporary repositories' and that we clearly feel the need to preserve our environment for our use and enjoyment and to transmit it 'in good shape' to forthcoming generations; to understand that we can and must make efficient use of the natural resources at our disposal, but with an awareness to their replacement value, at least, to transfer the management of the heritage received as a thrilling challenge. Today, a large part of humanity understands this, shares it and freely communicates it as an obligatory daily mission.

It seems that we have legislated, as yet without too much success, against excessive pollution emission, against generating polluting waste or its uncontrolled disposal. Many of us do not wish to do business with companies that practise uncontrolled production methods as a sign of our total disagreement. A similar step forward took place with companies using child labour or over-exploiting timetables and salaries in Third World countries.

We note with concern and a certain passiveness that we are losing much of what humanizes us, and we are becoming more and more distanced from what is really important to us. We seem to have inverted our scale of values in such a way that we are stressed, depressed and worried . . . and we stress, depress and worry our associates, customers, suppliers, friends and closest relatives.

The short-term result is low productivity, a reduction in the capacity for commitment, the disappearance of creativity and the capacity for innovation. The mid-term result is the gradual migration of 'the best' professionals to other companies and sometimes to the competition, and an inability to attract and hire talented staff at reasonable prices.

The pollution caused by stress, lack of motivation, the abandonment of the essential household tasks such as caring for children and the elderly, the supervised upbringing of adolescents, the hours of affective contact between the members of the family in favour of almost exclusive dedication to professional activities has a cost. This pollution is not quantified today, just as years ago no appraisal was made of the cost of 'dirty' kilowatts, the overuse of water or the lack of waste management.

The cost of overuse translates into a great loss of productivity for one and all: for the company, which has less creativity and commitment; for society, which loses well-rounded people and transforms them into workaholics with high health and social costs; and expenses for the individual, who might lose his or her own life meaning.

The inability of the welfare state to absorb the costs of this 'pollution' reveals the responsibility of the company before the human ecology that is bearing this impact. Table 5.1 presents four different types of companies according to their effects on human ecology.

We must therefore reconsider the company so that it might be an institution that continues to fulfil its specific mission of generating and sharing wealth, but without losing sight of its overall mission: to

Table 5.1 Four different types of company and their effect on human ecology

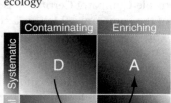

develop all its components towards excellence. The business policies that help to harmonize work and family, social and personal life, are only a first step towards guaranteeing productivity, fairness and survival. These policies becoming common practice in each company depends on the senior management that designs policies and sets an example; on the employees who, whenever required, ask for them to be applied; and on the middle management, which agrees to apply them in specific daily cases.

We must all be agents of change before this systematically polluting, blind reality, in order to turn it into a systematically enriching reality not only for our pocketbooks, but also for our minds and hearts. In short, we must be agents of a sustainable reality and future.

Let us examine the phases that transform a company that is externally and internally structurally polluting into a company that is structurally enriching:

Raising awareness of and identify the problems.
Developing family-responsible business policies.
Developing a plan with specific solutions; integrating work/family in the strategy and culture of the company; that is, in the daily reality.

The Certification of Family Responsible Companies is one of the pioneering initiatives in Europe that could only have become what it is today thanks to the research effort carried out by IESE in this field within the corporate world and thanks to the support of the Ministry of Labour and Social Affairs and the +Family Foundation.

The Family Responsible Company Certificate is framed within the social responsibility of the company, which, as a corporation forming part of society, has rights and obligations that it must harmonize with its specific mission of creating wealth. Therefore, the certificate will seek:

- To harmonize the rights of the individual and those of the company
- To also satisfy the new stakeholder: the employee's family
- To promote respect for plurality, private life and the health of employees and the environment
- To analyse, correct and demonstrate a commitment to resolving inequalities, seeking measures of subsidiarity or collaboration with the public administrations in caring for dependent people.

The goal is to seek a standard and a model of certification for companies that attests to the fulfilment of minimal actions in factors related to conciliation of the family and professional life through family-responsible business policies and practices. The following are proposed:

- To implement these policies in the company
- To standardize a means of achieving it
- To create the first certificate in this area
- To define the auditing criteria used to implement this recognition.

With all of this, we do not intend to make a classification or a list of the 'good and bad', business-wise, given the fact that it is an option that is freely chosen or not at the helm of companies. Nor is our proposal intended to invade the terrain of labour rights established by sector-specific collective agreements. It merely attempts to provide the market (companies and customers) with a common tool of strategic innovation that is easily adaptable to the size and nature of the company (from SMEs to large multinationals, including as well public and non-governmental administrations) which clearly differentiates, and the ongoing improvement of businesses with positive consequences for one and all.

The Family Responsible Business Model© constitutes a guideline for evaluating or diagnosing a company in order to know at what stage it is. Four elements are examined (see Table 5.2).

Table 5.2   The family-responsible business model

1 Policies		2 Facilitators		
Job flexibility	Professional support	Leadership	Communication	4 Results
Family services	Non-salary benefits	Responsibility	Strategy	
3 Culture: Hindrances/Promoters				

Family-responsible policies are explained above; Family-responsible facilitators are the following:

- Leadership: Family-responsible organizations have managers who establish and communicate a clear direction for their organization and unite and motivate the other managers and mid-level managers so that through their behaviour they might serve as an example for their associates. They openly recognize the importance of reconciling work and family life as a basis for the success of the business and integrate this focus to build a climate of support.
- Communication: The need to internally and externally communicate policies, instructions, objectives and targets is common to all organizations and is an important working tool through which individuals understand and assume their role in the organization. To consistently and effectively promote the family-responsible culture through communication thus becomes a requisite for the success of formal policies.
- Responsibility: For an organization to change, it is critical that individuals become responsible for both the implementation of formal policies and their use. The family-responsible culture is built on the basis of the trust, maturity and professionalism of everyone involved.
- Strategy: The organization's commitment to creating a culture that encourages and develops a balance between work and family is fundamental. By devoting time, personnel and resources to these initiatives and including respect for the family in the mission, the company's vision and values constitute clear signs of change.

The family-responsible impediments and stimuli existing in a business culture somehow condition the success and proper implementation of family-responsible policies. In some cases these practices destroy any attempt by employees to balance work with family life, such as the practice of staying on late at work because the bosses also stay on.

The family responsible results that measure the true impact of the three previous elements on the organization, namely: the degree of employee awareness concerning the different policies introduced and the elements present in the company culture; the frequency with which such policies are used by the employees; and the level of conflict between work and family experienced by the employees and their intention to leave the company for this reason.

In recent times, labour requirements have become very demanding. Some companies have obliged their employees to postpone their personal life to a future that never arrives and, what is worse, to reject it in order to replace it with working life, which is absurd. Amongst many other possibilities, here we describe the issues that should sound the alarm in any institution or company, because they are symptoms that something is going wrong:

- An excessive number of meetings, particularly those where there is a great deal of discussion yet no specific agreement is reached
- Well-developed plans and projects that very rarely come to fruition
- Rewarding anybody who stays on two or three hours after leaving time
- Expecting all executives or managers to be available at any time of day, for which they are obliged to be contactable wherever they go (mobile phone, beeper, and so on)
- Receiving official electronic messages written late at night or early in the morning and/or at the weekend (which should be spent on family life) and/or from holiday or rest places with the expectation that they be answered immediately
- A very high divorce rate amongst the upper-level employees or managers
- Workers' relatives (mainly their wives and children) complaining about the excessive amount of time they devote to the company
- Work being the only subject of discussion or conversation in meetings where several people from the same company get together

- Workers realizing that going to the cinema, theatre, opera, concerts, museums or entertainment centres has become an exceptional activity in their life
- Work becoming overwhelming and causing more stress than satisfaction for the person doing it.

Along with corporate effort and the commitment of managers who have changed, we must add the explicit will and complicity of the employees. We have already previously said that the company is unable to protect the worker from himself. So where is the key? In personal leadership. Corporate governance is facilitated when each person, when each employee, has a clear idea of his or her personal mission and acts with coherence and personal leadership.

6
The Secret of Personal Leadership

'Whoever has a positive mind remains immune to illness.'

Thomas Hamblin

'Living for others is not only the law of duty, it is also the law of happiness.'

Auguste Comte

An old Arab tale says that on one occasion the old Sufi, Bayacid, said to his disciples, 'When I was young, I was a revolutionary, and my prayer consisted of saying to God, "Give me the strength to change the world." But later, as I became an adult, I realized that I had not changed a single soul. Then my prayer began to be, "Lord, give me the grace to transform those who are in contact with me, even though it might only be my family". And now that I am old, I am beginning to realize how stupid I have been, and my only prayer is, "Lord give me the strength to change myself." And I think that if I had prayed this from the start, I would not have wasted my life.'

Our role as decision-makers in day-to-day life is the key to personal leadership. This ability, which is also called self-possession, self-control or even self-leadership, only makes sense when there is a purpose that is worth it. Nobody is attracted, at least not for long, by effort based on 'duty for duty's sake'. When a person discovers his or her personal mission in life, it not only includes what profession he wants to undertake but also the person he wants to love and continue to love; only then he is capable of specifying this purpose in the roles and priorities that materialize in a thousand activities each day which, though costly at times, are worthwhile, because they serve the fundamental objective. This idea, which is useful when dealing practically with time management (whoever has a reason is the one who gets out of bed each morning) serves for us to be able to focus our lives.

Self-leadership is also absolutely necessary to be able to lead others in the different realms of our lives (children's upbringing, social co-existence, teamwork and company management) and is a basic condition for being happy. Women, whose ambition is to fully live their personal and working lives, need to start with a self in which the mission, role and priorities form a complete, conscious, free and responsible whole. A person who leads his or her life is not one who chooses a path associated with success by others, but one who has a clear purpose and is capable of choosing the best path to follow in each case:

> I found it difficult to realize that performance is not a single model for everyone and is not set out in a manual or in the life of film stars. To be the boss of one's own life involves constantly deciding, acting to achieve what you think you should achieve, being able not to set any role in our lives aside, and to accomplish this it is necessary to prioritize time and again.
>
> (journalist, mother of three)

This self-leadership is therefore nourished by competencies, by virtues or values in action, such as self-awareness, emotional intelligence, proactiveness, time and stress management, management of one's personal and professional career, and affective maturity.

The degree of development of these competences is what determines a person's level of *personal leadership* and therefore their ability to generate healthy relationships with others, thus making them capable of becoming a leader for them in a natural way as a result of the innate prestige they exert on others. Competencies are therefore the roots that enable our life to give forth abundant fruit. If we are not capable of running our own lives, how are we going to be capable of leading other people?

As the old saying goes, 'Nobody can give what they do not have'. It is imperative to constantly improve this set of competencies, which begins with self-awareness and which is forged in cautious decision-making based on self-control, integrity and proactiveness. It is necessary to pass from the state of unawareness (where we do not even perceive the need to improve or change) to the state of action (where people know where to direct their efforts and are capable of doing so):

> Being a minority, feeling that you have to show that you are also 100 per cent when you're pregnant or your child is sick, viewing the working rules as still male and being required to play along with them ... are circumstances which have made me grow as a woman in two competencies that I believe are sort of our speciality: perseverance and time management.
>
> (management secretary, one child)

However, it is not sufficient to design one's professional life; it is also necessary to foresee, to anticipate our life, otherwise problems appear suddenly and sometimes dramatically to intelligent women who have overcome all other professional or social barriers but find that they are losing control of their family life. We must not forget that life involves constant dynamism and that the absence of development almost always suggests a retreat. Just like wines, with time we either become a 'grand reserve' or we turn into vinegar, and this also happens with interpersonal relationships. Whatever does not grow, dies:

> I was wrong in thinking that things that are achieved do not have to be maintained. After several years of a happy marriage with three lovely children, my husband told me he was leaving. I had devoted a lot of time in the previous year to my promotion in the company. It is not only about simply avoiding the *not now, darling*, but taking care of communication and sharing everything honestly.
>
> (area manager, two daughters)

But on what does this capacity to improve, to learn and develop skills, competences and values depend? Fundamentally on *attitude*, not only towards work or the organization of which we form a part, but also towards our own life, which may be either a powerful engine or a virtually insurmountable obstacle, depending on how we approach it:

I have always wanted to get to the top, not to be happy with the well-beaten tracks; difficulty is a challenge for me. This has pushed me on at the hardest times.

(managing director)

Emotional intelligence

Daniel Goleman coined the term 'emotional intelligence'[1] to designate an essential competence for anyone who has to manage people: the *capacity to manage one's emotions*, a task that actually lasts one's entire lifetime. More than twenty-five centuries ago, Aristotle said that we are all capable of becoming angry, but that very few of us are capable of getting angry at the right time, with the right person, for the right reason, in the right tone...

Goleman has made the term EI a classic, encompassing five groups of basic emotional skills: awareness of oneself (recognizing our own feelings), self-control (being capable of regulating ourselves), self-motivation (being proactive in the most diverse situations), empathy (recognizing the feelings of others) and social skills (suitably handling our relations with others). Men, at least, are outstanding in self-control, women in empathy and social skills. Today, research from MIT gives scientific support to these intuitions: they have a physiological basis. Here, too, in the development of the emotional intelligence of a manager and a company, it is possible to talk of complementariness:

> Men do not personalize conflicts, and they are capable of arguing and then continuing to work together. They argue about an issue, not the involvement or the point of view that each of them has, and this enables them to have greater control over their emotions, because they do not spill over from one realm to the other (from the personal to the professional or the other way round). However, we cannot avoid always seeing specific people with personal stories. When faced with a specific human being, we do not become abstract but go into depth. We reach reality intuitively.
>
> (publisher, four children)

Here it is necessary to stress the importance of two kinds of intelligence that go beyond the classical IQ and which are the basis for true leadership: intrapersonal intelligence (my relationship with myself) and interpersonal intelligence (my relationship with others). Goleman stresses that as we advance towards the higher echelons in an organization, a leader's effectiveness is ever more closely linked to the possession of both of these kinds of intelligences.

Once more the question arises as to how we achieve them. Maturity, repetitions of conscious acts along certain lines ... To wit, a few years ago the well-known management guru Stephen Covey,[2] pointed to two sets of habits needed to become mature adults and generate healthy relationships with others. First we must achieve a 'private victory', the objective of which is to shift from being *dependent* on the environment (the paradigm of you) to becoming autonomous (he says *independent*), the paradigm of the self. To do this, he suggests being proactive, beginning with a specific purpose in mind and doing first things first. Then comes the 'public victory' (thinking of winning/winning, seeking synergies and first seeking to understand and then to be understood). Through this we come to habits which allow us to become *interdependent* (the paradigm of we). The maximum expression of interdependence lies in the family, and therefore, without this basic core of socialization and education in values, it would be impossible to achieve a healthy society with values and maturity.

Maybe this is what might explain the results of certain recent research on stress and work–family conciliation.[3] Here, it is obvious that the multiplicity of roles (professional, father, brother, friend ...) does not diminish one's self-realization and satisfaction, nor does it lower concentration on one task or another, because given the affective and intellectual structure of human beings, certain activities recharge from others and vice versa. Tension is caused by a lack of time to do everything (unfavourable social and business environment, incompatibility of work, commercial and family timetables, etc.), not because there are incompatible realities inside the person. As we saw in Chapter 3, the family and life after work are undoubtedly a true, authentic school of competencies.

Wanting is being able

This entire set of skills requires the acquisition of the habit of proactiveness as a result of the constant, rational effort to use freedom when faced with any stimulus, since what is characteristic of humans is their rationality, that is, their ability to respond to their surroundings by overcoming them and not giving in like animals, the tendency of which is usually the same when faced with a specific circumstance. Humans are capable of saying no, of delaying the satisfaction of their instincts (unlike animals) depending on other higher interests. Proactiveness somehow leads us to anticipate circumstances and act in consequence. Therefore, a good way to discover whether or not we are proactive or reactive to the environment is by questioning on what we spend our time and energy.

We all have a load of things that concern us: health, children, work, inflation...even world hunger or the threat of international terrorism. This is what Covey[4] calls our *circle of concern*. When we review the things lying inside this circle, it is obvious that we have no real control over some of them, whereas we are able to do something about others. If we contain the latter into a sub-unit of the former, we have our *circle of influence*. Distinguishing each area entails paving the way to proactiveness, since in this way it will be easier to apply our efforts to matters that we are able to change:

> Getting obsessed about something is always an impediment. To avoid this, there is nothing like action, but preceded by a reflection on things that we can do and which are within our reach. Being a mother has helped me to view things relatively more than any other professional or social situation, more than any discourse on priorities. I think that any person devoted to others, either compulsorily (motherhood) or by personal choice, is better prepared to distinguish what is important for me now and what is not.
>
> (investment analyst, one daughter)

Truly proactive (not activist) people focus their efforts on their circle of true influence, and as a result of the energy that permeates them, this circle grows incessantly. At the same time, the issues lying within the circle of concerns (which they are unable to influence) are reduced.

On the other side, reactive people focus their efforts on the circle of concern (others' faults, world problems and other circumstances over which they have no control whatsoever). This gives rise to anguish, feelings of guilt and impotence. All of this, combined with a lack of attention to the areas where they can do something, leads them to reduce their circle of influence (by allowing things that are not inside the circle to fill their mind and waste their energy):

> The most arduous things become possible when, once we realize they are feasible, we do them. Putting off matters makes them more and more difficult. On the contrary, dealing with them at the right time increases our abilities and might even make the other phantasms that so concern us vanish.
>
> (self-employed businesswoman, no children)

The circle of concern is full of 'haves' (if I had a good boss, if I had a bigger house, if I had a doctorate, if I had an easier child, if I had . . .). The circle of influence is full of 'bes' (I can be more patient, affectionate, be more sensible, more creative, more co-operative . . .). If we think the problem is out there and give it the power to control us, we are lost. However, our happiness does not have to depend on changing what lies outside; let us begin by changing ourselves, our attitude; let us work on our faults, let us be different and then we will lay the groundwork to be able to bring about a positive change in our surroundings. In fact, the greatest asset of all men and women is their character.

On choosing our response to circumstances, we have a powerful influence over them and become capable of influencing an ever broader circle. To direct this effort and all those that lead to improving our personal development, we must focus on what is *feasible* at all times.

Motivational conflicts and learning

We are not determined but merely conditioned by nature or the environment. Human beings are focuses of freedom, we have inner freedom, and this differentiates us from the animal kingdom. But for freedom to be functional, it must be exercised through rationality, judging on each occasion what should be done and not allowing ourselves to be carried away by what we most fancy at any given time.[5] In fact, these times of conflict between what I would like to do and what I rationally see as best are when we stake our degrees of future freedom on the following decision. Let us examine this point in more detail.

The *reasons* a person uses in their decisions are the true *values in action*, regardless of the values one claims to have. The nature of these reasons is also related to the values themselves. But recall that there are three kinds of reasons behind human action, all necessary and all mutually complementary: (1) *extrinsic* reasons, which drive the action from outside the person by means of incentives such as money or praise; (2) *intrinsic* reasons, which drive the action from inside the person, such as learning or satisfaction at a job well done; and (3) *transcendent* reasons, which encourage the action from inside a person because of a benefit for another person, such as knowing that one's own action satisfies the true needs of others.

Why do values that seemed objective and unchangeable for a certain culture, collective or civilization change? Each generation is marked not only by the values it proclaims, but by the appraisals it makes of these values, in other words, by the subjective appraisal of these values made in line with the upbringing and, therefore, of the specific appreciation that each person shows when facing a certain reality. Things attract us or do not attract us depending on the appraisal we make of reality. This is when we recognize the reasons or criteria that we take into account in any decision. Furthermore, the motivational force that leads us to action may be spontaneous or rational. If the motivation driving a person is less and less rational, there is a danger that counter values will be forged as objectives. The danger of acting, motivated perhaps by deceit or irrationality, is what is theoretically a value for the person and will no longer be primary in the decision process. Individuals end up being slaves to a spontaneous motivation that is removed from all external stimuli that the environment might present. It is therefore this and not the person that holds the reins to one's life.

Intermotivational conflict arises when our spontaneous drive impels us towards what is attractive in the action for extrinsic reasons, whereas reason gives us the negative consequences that this action will have on others. We often forget that a reason ignored in one decision loses strength in later decisions. What we fail to choose will 'appeal to us less and less'. This is the force of habit and the formation of virtues (positive habits) and vices (negative habits). If we allow ourselves to be carried away by what we like, we might reach the 'Scrooge effect', referring to the miser in Dickens's classical Christmas tale, where it is more and more difficult to foresee and assess the consequences of one's actions on others, because one's reasons are more and more selfish.

The family, the company and society need people capable of harmoniously bringing together the three types of reasons: extrinsic, intrinsic and transcendent. The *motivational quality* of a person, in other words what is most humane, is the result of their range of reasons and depends on the extent to which they have learnt to consider their transcendent reasons and how they affect their actions or omissions with respect to others. For example, an intermediary who sells to earn a commission and is also driven by a desire to grow in the face of the different professional challenges by also serving the true needs of the customers, has a greater motivational quality than one who also works as an intermediary but only seeks the largest commission for himself, even at the expense of deceiving the customer. When motivational quality is richest, the intermediary is capable of experiencing satisfaction on the three levels of needs. Furthermore, in the long run, an individual motivated only by extrinsic and intrinsic motivations will end up 'burnt out' by the activity, since despite making his utmost efforts, he will not manage to satisfy his most essential needs.

People who discuss these conflicts and make decisions by only paying attention to one of three levels of human needs (material, knowledge and affective), end up suffering a 'defeat' that produces personal *dissatisfaction* and *frustration*. The question is how to resolve this conflict. In the interviews conducted, we frequently heard the phrase, 'I can't do everything...choosing a good career involves a sacrifice.' When this type of conflict is resolved in favour of the working world, a negative balance is generally given. However, it is interesting to see that people who have slowed up their professional life for personal reasons are not usually sorry to have done so. Furthermore, anyone who waives all objective recognition, although they might subjectively feel happy (either due to the kind of work they have chosen or because they devote their lives to their family) sooner or later will have a self-esteem crisis. All human beings need to satisfy the three types of reasons and in doing so receive the dose of recognition (social, affective, professional, economic) that each case or situation requires:

> That company no longer interested me, I was only there while I looked for something else. As a result of this situation, I was more and more capable of putting up with anything. I ended up burnt out.
>
> (graphic designer, single)

This is the reason why neither the purely 'selfish' intermediary (the one motivated spontaneously by extrinsic reasons), nor the purely 'altruist' intermediary (the one spontaneously motivated by transcendent reasons) will last long in a business, and why the 'burn-out' rate is so high. Neither approach is realistic.

In short, when faced with intermotivational currents in our daily lives, if we are led round spontaneous desires (towards the appeal of action), we will become more and more slaves to our own tastes (tastes, too, must be educated). We would then enter the dynamic of what is called 'negative learning' or the 'vicious cycle,' which involves being more hooked on everything related to 'having' (power, fame, material goods and so forth).

The alternative dynamic is rational, that of 'positive learning' or the 'virtuous circle'. Here we are capable of reducing our current freedom of decision-making in order to expand our freedom of decision-making tomorrow; in other words, acting in this way makes us capable of satisfactorily putting off current, immediate actions in favour of the benefits of an inner change that will enable us to enjoy higher levels of effectiveness and satisfaction in the future. This learning process is anchored in 'being', having things as the means (in their fair measure) to serve others and ourselves. This is the process that humanizes people and gives them the necessary strength and temperament for others to recognize their moral authority and leadership. In fact, it allows them to have a good relationship with their surroundings, fully entering the whole paradigm of what a person is. The more coherent the person is with the correct principles according to reason, the more capable they will be of perceiving reality and therefore the more effective they will be as positive agents of change.

Affective maturity

As we saw in the previous section, being a person means having material, cognitive and affective needs. Likewise, the process of learning, leading to humanization inevitably involves developing affection. But the first step of this affective maturity (what a paradox!) lies with reason: since I rationally perceive others as complete people, I act accordingly and I internalize the model, which harmoniously develops my affective side. Affection is thus developed by entering others' worlds, by going outside oneself and one's own needs:

When we were married but did not have children, you really couldn't talk about conflict. Our relationship was very similar to when we were going out together. When the children arrived we had to change our habits and timetables and give up part of our freedom, relieve the other of their obligations or simply share them. We knew each other more in difficulty. Although it was hard at the beginning, the truth is that our love matured.

(married couple aged 37 and 33, two children)

The culture around us (from the media to novels and television series) seems to encourage us to think that feelings should be the *cause* of our actions. However, this would mean only allowing our emotions to take over instead of developing ourselves into whole people with heads and hearts. In fact, reality has shown us that this 'handing over the reins' is made up of an affective map in what at times we do not recognize ourselves. The fact is that feelings are the *result* of our actions (or omissions).

The learning process for developing an affective approach therefore begins with wanting (rationally) to *do something* for others for whom maybe now we do not feel anything positive (although perhaps we had felt it previously).

But this 'something' must be something *feasible, achievable* for us (each person will know how high this step may be to negotiate), something which involves our making an effort to escape from what spontaneously appeals to us at the time (to ignore someone or even treat them badly), and to follow the determinations of our heart which indicate what is easiest in this circumstance. If we take this step and we put our thoughts into action, the result is that our capacity to feel something positive for this person will grow. 'Acting is the best form of loving. We do not have to feel love for others, but simply to help them, and you'll see how quickly you love them.'[6]

The greatest of all values is love, but as Susana Tamaro reminds us in her book *Follow your Heart*, 'True love is not always felt; it is practised.' Although the family, the affective bonds of all human beings come first, they often end up in last place due to a lack of dedication, and they thus risk being lost. In the family, in the company, in society, human relationships are built on a daily basis from inside each person.

Reason enables us to discover how to use power, how to withstand adversity, and at the same time how to struggle to improve it, but above all it illuminates reality, making us discover people instead of human roles. Given our physiology and natural tendency to motherhood (real or potential), this is one of women's strengths. However, it is easy to fall into the sentimentality that removes us from an objective view of reality. To be agents of change, we must know how to use our heads and hearts well.

The stages in the process for affective development would therefore be the following: I rationally perceive the value of others, I effectively want to do something and make this influence my decisions, I do it and as a result my virtue and feeling grows; in other words, I become more human and also lay the base for the other, if he or she wishes (they are free beings) to change or improve their feelings towards me. This is the principle of reciprocity in human relations. It is the rational love that is born out of will and grows with acts of devotion.

Success and personal life

Women can teach men that success is not always associated with formal power. We tend more to seek influence (informal power) and to work on something we enjoy alongside people with whom we get on. This is why we can become experts at forming teams.

(psychologist, four children)

I have always wanted to get to the top, I like to take things to the limit, I like to work, but what truly changed my mental puzzle and my priorities was motherhood.

(managing director, three daughters)

So many years in second place in a multinational and I lost a suitcase on a trip to India which made me reflect. I am single, I have dedicated myself to work, but the truth is that I have no time to spend the money I earn or to develop friendships and relationships. I live for my job. I do not want to suffer from stress, depression or anxiety alone in a hotel room.

(multinational manager, single)

These testimonies are a very accurate X-ray of the concept of success and the pressure this imposes on people. Being successful is rewarding and desirable, and it is also something natural in human beings.

People have always aspired to rise, as Gregorio Marañón said, every-body must stand out in something specific in everything that surrounds them and compared to themselves in previous situations.[7] The problem lies in measuring success and the pressure of success on people's lives.

Today, everyone is subject to measurements of efficiency and eval-uation of their work, and the triumphs and failures are virtually public. This is the new phenomenon of *notoriety* built under the aus-pices of the media, and it is linked to the idea that success must be individual (*self-made men and women*). The important thing is personal determination, and therefore the reasoning is, 'My main interest is myself. Freedom consists of defining my life as I like . . . / . . . But I must demonstrate to myself that *I am of value and I am someone. By demonstrating what I am, I am successful.*'[8]

However, in order to delve into this subject, it is first necessary to define the *objective and subjective dimensions of success*. Objective success (measurable) is defined by external parameters. This basically includes fame and recognition (social, economic, professional, returned love). In contrast, subjective success is defined by inner criteria, visible to others only through behaviour. This entails feeling good with oneself, which comes from coherence with our value system.

Social pressure sometimes makes it very difficult *to choose, and we adhere to the stereotypes, we live by the guidelines set by others*. This causes relative happiness in which we might adopt one of two stances: we might feel forlorn, because the effort does not come from the challenges and is therefore agreed, or we might react critically. This involves fairly evaluating the influence of training, the environ-ment, the trends and being able to surpass the environment through an active world of personal values.

But what can damage our self-esteem? What is psychologically called 'self-concept', or the idea we have of ourselves and which in some way is independent of our actions and at times even transcends them. An excessively demanding self-concept may destroy sufficient self-esteem. Our upbringing, fashion or social stereotypes can create, modify or accentuate this self-concept and lead to a conflict. If our self-concept is rigid, it can damage our self-esteem and prevent us from being happy. This situation has a great deal to do with success. Self-concept taken to an extreme lies exclusively in the world of objective success: 'What they expect of me is this, and I accept it as ideal.' From the definition of subjective and objective success, we can

Table 6.1 Four types of people and life situations

		Objective success	
		+	−
Subjective Success	+	Model	Realized
	−	Famou	Failed

establish a table where these two concepts are the basic co-ordinates. By combining them, we can see interesting types of people and life situations (see Table 6.1).

REALIZED. This a person who, despite not having achieved the visible results associated with external recognition (objective success) in life, is aware that his or her value system and affective life is solid and alive (subjective success). They are happy and at peace with themselves.

MODEL. This is the case of people who have as much internal as external success. We have called them models because in some way they are referents for those around them. This situation, though possible and real, does not often occur or last for a long time, because life is constantly changing and there is a risk of one easily falling into the following quadrant, which we will call 'famous'.

FAMOUS. Here we have a group of people which on many occasions are set forth as models, but, despite the objective success of their lives (money, awards, promotions, returned love) whose inner life, their world of motivations, does not satisfy them and they are in permanent crisis with their self-concept and therefore with their self-esteem.

FAILED. This would be a person who, given a lack of objective results (objective success) squanders their interior world (subjective success), or vice versa.

The whole of this scenario contains the idea of *recognition*. It is very easy to go from being a 'model' to being 'famous', because the external recognition (objective success) may make the person more superficial and frivolous, with the resulting loss of values. It can also occur that people in the 'realized' quadrant might pass to 'failed', as it is not possible for a long time, and less still all one's life, to withstand a total absence of external recognition, as a loss of self-esteem will be the inexorable result.

Despite everything, success in achievements helps us to see the efficiency of our work and encourages us to take on new jobs. Success is dynamic and ephemeral by essence; it has to be won every day. If someone hopes to be successful, they run the risk of suffering, of committing terrible mistakes to achieve it.

Personal success is the result of 'doing something that fills our lives'.[9] What can fill the lives of parents and professionals of the 21st century? One of the first points to consider is *having a fear of failure*, first of professional failure, which is the most visible of all. Failure accepted with a reflective spirit teaches us the path to success better than success itself. In Europe we do not have this mentality; we dress up reality. We forget that overcoming a failure may be a guarantee for success later on.

Another interesting matter is that of *knowing how to manage success*. There is what Hermann Simon calls 'leaders in the shadows',[10] people who have managed to avoid the difficulties of a disorderly not well-managed triumph and who have avoided the giddiness of tyrannical success. They have managed to detect the dangers of external success in time, but to be able to do this, one must know clearly that personal triumph is the product of a successful life.

The success of women and the family

Today women, just like men, must overcome the challenges that the company or professional organization requires and assigns to them. Whether or not they achieve this depends on their respective successes. Here we find the first stumbling block: 'their respective successes'. Where does the family, the common project, end up? They often do not have time to share their plans, to talk, and also the child-rearing and housework require greater attention.

Sometimes, when considering the consequences on family life of the situation created by *the culture of success*, we come up against the temptation to advise that success should be renounced in benefit of the family, but this is not the best scenario. Rather instead of renouncing success, it is a question of being successful in line with our family and professional plans, so that they might even feed each other instead of complaining that one is an obstacle to the other.

Yet are we capable of doing this? Do we have the right mindset to achieve professional success and fulfil our family responsibilities? All of us are like Chinese jugglers who try to keep many plates in the air, ensuring that none fall down. They are all important, but only one is made of porcelain, the family. The others are made of plastic and are therefore 'replaceable'.

The problem is that, in addition to wanting all of our activities to be compatible, sometimes we want to be perfect tens in them all. This is when we say, 'It is not possible to have everything at the same time.' When we say this, are we not just finding a reason why we have sacrificed family life or our marriage in favour of social or professional success (or the other way round)? But to what extent is this true? Is it not more accurate to say that we are rejecting the idea of thinking with perspective and designing our life careers by includ-ing plateaux and breaks in accordance with the priorities of the moment? Might it not be that we find it difficult not to shine given the current parameters of measurement?

This, like everything, merits a few moments of pondering. If we do not reflect on our own life, what do we think about then? A good exercise, though very simple, is to define and write down our targets for the coming six months, 12 months, five years, etc. Let us trust this simple 'recipe'; let us get it underway and later we will evaluate the results.

Despite having taken on joint responsibility in family and working life, women may sometimes feel the social pressure that their dignity requires them to have paid work out of the home, and that this will help them to gain the respect even of their husbands! The result is, 'I will be happy if I work outside the home. If I always work outside the home, regardless of what happens. If I stand out there.' However, we see that this is not always the case. Rather we should be saying, 'I will be happy if I work on a project suited to my desires, to my personal and family needs and in accordance with our common goals.' All of this must take into account the fact that an effort is required from everyone to value and recognize the housework, because as said before, nobody is capable of living and feeling fulfilled without objective recognition.

At other times, the conflict arises in the opposite situation. Many women also wish to work outside the home, but the social rigidity, the rigidity of the company or even the traditional assignment of roles can make it unthinkable for her to consider taking a job and for the man to stay at home. The desirable thing would then be to be able to decide within a framework of freedom, common sense and mutual communication, and to do so in line with a very important, perhaps the most important, factor: the children and their specific needs at each stage in their lives.

This is how it is possible to achieve total success, which is nothing more than the sum of personal, professional, social and family success. We can triumph in all of these domains if we do not ignore any of them and if we have a very clear idea of our mission, roles and priorities and try to act in consonance with it. Female ambition is to achieve overall success that fulfils the different roles and facets of life. In the following chapter we will go further into the basic tool to make this overall success, that is, true female ambition, a reality in our day-to-day life. As Flaubert said, 'The past is a corpse and the future is unknown, but we often turn to them and thus waste energy to live fully in the present, the only time we actually have and upon which we can act.' It is easy to fall into this trap, but it is not so difficult to get out of it. Time management is the main competency of truly efficient people, those that lead their own lives.

7
Managing Personal, Family and Professional Time: How to Accomplish Everything

'The small things that are accomplished are better than all the large things that are planned.'

George Marshall

'I wasted my time, now time is wasting me.'

Shakespeare

Time thieves

The use of time defines the interests of a person fairly well. We have time for what we are really interested in, but we do not recognize it very often. What is more, it is not precisely the person claiming to be busy who makes best use of their time, rather the one who manages to set aside suitable times for each thing.

Time is an atypical, equitable (we all have time while we live and every day has 24 hours), inelastic, essential good; it is an essential life co-ordinate alongside space, which is irreplaceable and inexorable (it goes by and nobody has managed to stop it at a specific point). Our life is also characterized as being immersed in an overwhelming flow of information and technological developments that can make it yet more difficult for us to make effective use of time. We constantly have to choose.

Paraphrasing Drucker, we can say that 'nothing distinguishes an efficient person as well as their love of time'.[1] For anybody wanting to take the reins of their life, it is essential for them to know where their time is being systematically invested or wasted, to help them discover the so-called 'time thieves'. Because if we are not the lords of our own time, is there anything else we can master? A good exercise to achieve this objective consists of noting every two hours throughout a whole week what you have done during this period. This gives us important information, an objective diagnosis of what to begin to build and therefore to improve in our time management. This simple practice will help us to differentiate our perception of what we do and do not do in reality very well. In fact, it consists of managing our lives.

There have always been time thieves and there always will be. Napoleon said that there are thieves who are not punished even though they might steal what is most important to us, our time. The problem is not a new one, though maybe in this century we are experiencing it more acutely. But what are actually the causes of our time losses? Perhaps we might think that we lack information, that communications in the company are slow and absurd, that there are constant interruptions, disorganization of our closest associates, too much rushing, telephone calls, mistakes made by others, excessive bureaucracy, long, useless meetings...even a certain incompetence among the bosses. But...what if we look at ourselves first? For this is the only reality that we are able to change. We will surely find a lack of personal organization, muddled priorities, little delegation to co-workers, excessive optimism in assessing our own skills and working potential, an intention to cover an excessively broad field of activity, lack of punctuality and control of one's timetable, delay or excessive haste in important decisions, etc.

In fact, the most frightening *time thieves* are generally internal, and there are usually three of them:

- *Not knowing how to say no*:

  Now I regret my total availability with the company. After six years, I decided to have a child and my working situation has worsened. My leaving time, very late, created a precedent that now I am not able to change.

  (economist, one child)

- *Not knowing how to delegate*:

  I do the shopping myself, the maid cannot do it, the household economy depends on this.

  (doctor, four children)

It is impossible with my husband, I cannot talk about sharing the chores with him. I do it better by myself.

(university professor, three children)

- *Abdicating the responsibility for important matters*:

If I regret anything, it is having left my children's upbringing in the hands of strangers. The level of my life and my income paradoxically have not served to give them a better upbringing. I feel that I have abdicated.

(marketing manager, two children)

Any of these three thieves are very bad for personal and professional time management. A person who does not know how to say no may be somewhat narcissistic and may therefore need to lead everything, although this activity might be exhausting in itself. They might also have a histrionic personality. Such people generally do not like to go down badly due to a lack of security and humility or are individuals with a hysterical personality who only seek to be liked. Finally, this category also includes those who, with good intentions, suffer from the 'saviour syndrome' and always strive to solve other's problems without realizing that this is impossible; it is not always possible to do everything. These people may break down due to lack of common sense, self-awareness and an ability to prioritize. We must bear in mind that in order to serve . . . the most important thing is being useful, in other words, to be prepared for it. Continuing with our system of priorities, we should avoid 'squandering' ourselves on specific situations or people. Since we are using our energies, we should do so for people or things that are worthwhile, and here, of course, our family comes into the spotlight.

Normally, when 'I am robbed' of time, the main cause lies within me because there is an external factor that claims my attention (telephone, visits) and the reply is always personal. I am the one who decides my priorities and the time I spend on each activity.

We can also be the cause of self-interruptions. To find out if we are part of this group, we need only answer in the affirmative to at least a few of these questions. Is my desk untidy? Do I sometimes extend my coffee or lunch breaks? Do I put things off? Do I often stop during the day to talk to others? Am I distracted by magazines or surfing on the Internet when I should be working on other things? Do I make private telephone calls or answer personal e-mails during working hours? As a result of these habits, it is highly likely that I am also the cause of interruptions in other people's work through unannounced or unplanned calls or visits. It is necessary to respect others' time so that they will respect ours.

Sometimes we think we are in control of time, but we actually suffer from some of its pathologies:

- *The urgency of today*, deceiving ourselves, living between the frenetic time of yesterday and the anguish for what we have not yet done; we let ourselves get carried away by what is urgent (the time being marked externally) instead of what is important (related directly to my system of priorities and its implementation at any given time).

  Doing what I have to do today is enough for me. I don't even manage to do what I am supposed to each day, so how can I expect to plan and anticipate events?

  (consultant, three children)

- *Low output*, perhaps because we manage it badly. Kipling talked about filling each minute with sixty intense seconds. As they cannot be stored or recovered, it is necessary to constantly make good use of time, but to do this we need to have decided beforehand where we are going because there is no tailwind for a wanderer.

  I don't understand how it is possible to be so tired and see that the output of my time is so low; I think that seeing this tires me even more than the work I have to do each day.

  (businesswoman in the tourist sector, two children)

- *Clashes between the use of time and personal goals.* We might make use of time but its use might not correspond to the objectives or goals that we had previously set. Henry Kissinger said, 'There is nothing more frustrating in life than setting an objective and watching time pass without achieving it.' And we add, 'It is even worse to struggle for this objective, attain it and then find that it wasn't worthwhile and was useless.'

It sometimes happens with my children, and also at work. I achieve certain things, but not what I saw as important or high priority at the outset.

(lawyer, two children)

In order to avoid the situations, we must never lose sight of these three laws of time:

The time required by a job grows in proportion to the number of times that we interrupt and restart it; therefore, let us always try to take natural breaks so that we stop at the end of each chapter, we work on a report to the end of the section, etc. These natural breaks will give us a sense of achievement, which then increases our energy. Furthermore, when we start the activity again we do not need to waste time trying to remember what the subject was about, and it is easier to 'warm up'.

It is much more difficult to plan and/or carry out a lengthy task than a short one. This obliges us to pinpoint reasonable times in our agenda, realistic times adapted to the situation we hope to achieve.

Sometimes there are jobs that are overwhelmingly large, that are put off and given low priority in short-term planning (a doctoral thesis, studying English...), and many people's reasoning is this: if the elephant is too large and my mouth is too small, it is better to put off the elephant until my mouth has grown enough. However, time passes and one's mouth does not grow; therefore, the elephant will never be digested, neither today nor later, and we run the risk of becoming burdened with our goal, of not achieving it, of blaming our circumstances: 'If I hadn't got married, if I hadn't had children...' It is more reasonable to face this enormous task for which we feel incapable and think of it as an exciting challenge that can be broken down and planned into realistic bits. This involves concentrating on digesting today's 'elephant fillet' and planning the rest, setting aside times on the agenda that allow us to go from one fillet to another until it is completely digested.

The value of a job does not grow in proportion to the time that is spent on it, but rather forms an 'S' curve. We should not fall into perfectionism, and nothing is better for avoiding this than establishing deadlines for performing that job that may always be improved.

Perfectionists have learnt to measure value itself in terms of their *achievements*, and as a result they are terrified of being average. Meanwhile, their non-perfectionist colleagues earn more money, pin down more important deals and ensure that things are done much faster. In these cases, it is necessary to start by recognizing that what is *less than acceptable* for a perfectionist is often perfectly acceptable for anybody else, and that it is essential to have a clear idea of the purpose of the task in order to be able to determine the time that should be put into it.

Let us forget the old saying, 'If you want something done well, do it yourself'. Do not ask yourself whether others could do the work *as well as* you. It is enough for them to do it well. Maybe they do it in a different way, but they might even do it better. A single person, depending on their tastes, interests and mood, might do some jobs lazily and be a perfectionist in others. Therefore, a good personal exercise is to decide beforehand how much time we are going to spend on each job depending on its difficulty and importance, not on our subjective desire to do it. In fact, if we do not establish limits, the following law is fulfilled: 'Any job consumes all the time available for its completion.' If we only have to write a letter, finish a report, or any other job, it can easily take up all the time we have and not the time it actually requires.

People who achieve their objectives are convinced that things done poorly give them the experience that will help them do better in the future. Thomas Edison tested more than a thousand filaments for electric light bulbs before finding one that worked. He said that he had not failed, but that he had been successful in discovering more than a thousand filaments that did not work. We must learn to look at errors as a step towards a future success.

Moreover, nothing is absolute. In fact, as somebody once said, 'Nothing ever happens, and if it does happen, does it matter, and if it matters, what's the problem?' To assess the true value of things that are very important to us, there are two key questions. How is this specific project going to fit into the rest of my life? What importance will it have in 150 years' time?

How to avoid overloading and stress

It is a harsh pace, but it suits my personality perfectly. I have always liked working to the limit, even when I was at school; now

in addition to variable timetables I have got involved in a foundation, which means I have to put in Saturday mornings and many
Tuesday afternoons.

My son is thirteen months old. I'm the one who gets him up
and puts him to bed at night. Before, if I had a lot of work, I used
to go to the office at 7 o'clock in the morning; now something
serious has to happen for me to do this.

My pregnancy was the best time of my life, I was euphoric and
worked harder and harder. My attitude caused my problems with
my husband, but in the end I was careful. I am a highly active
person and need very little rest, but I do unwind at weekends.

(consultant, mother of two)

Many of us could be victims of the so-called *Flapsi Hapsi*, or the
syndrome of active people who, despite their executive ability, do
not work according to a plan, but rather frenetically at the speed of
events. These are people who for long periods of time see all of their
future obligations (both at home and at work) as an unstructured,
disorganized mass of jobs. The big and small are mixed without any
order or concord. As a result, the brain is completely occupied
processing a multitude of unrelated small details, and it is impossible
to distinguish what is important from what is trivial. In such situations, many things are simply forgotten, others are carried out in an
irrational order, governed by bombarding impulses. One often chooses
to take extra work home or one enters a kind of paralysis or inertia
associated with a build-up of remorse. As a result, working priorities
are wrongly set because the external and internal disorder only allows
us to remember what is close at hand, and this situation may be
dangerous due to its influence on our overall view of things. When it
fails, one's energy and activity level is drastically reduced and so, too,
are our spontaneity and creativity. It is impossible for a head full of
loose ends to have the sense to actually control the situation.

Let us not forget that stress is often a subjective feeling of a lack of
control more than a real effect derived from more or less overwhelming
objective circumstances, although if it is experienced as such, it ends
up having psychosomatic consequences and causing illnesses (ulcers,
heart attacks, etc.).

Although there are many ways to get out of this situation, one of
them is as easy as noting down things that occur to us as pending

matters. The simple act of noting them considerably relieves the brain. It is important to transfer the matters on this list into our diary as soon as possible, with a specific date and time for each of the pending matters, noting them on master lists and distinguishing which could be delegated and which could be put off. A diary is like computer RAM memory and works in the same way, by downloading the content of a temporary memory which can then focus on other things. If we do not close this, if we do not use our diary efficiently, we will waste time resolving crises – in short, a dangerous vicious circle. A single diary then is much more than a reminder of appointments, it is a way to make a commitment to ourselves in things that we have deemed important in our life.

Knowing one's own limits and taking decisions in good time: sometimes we think that we can handle everything and we refuse to consider a change in our surroundings (reduced timetable, leave, reconsideration of daily priorities). This situation is not reached suddenly. There have surely been *daily instances of overloading* beforehand that have not been dealt with. These are the ones we can correct in time, and they also serve as training for hard situations. How do we face them?

- By counting up to five; we must relax and keep our mind cool
- By calmly checking what has to be done. Imagine that we are a military surgeon in an battle overwhelmed by the enormous number of wounded and by the limited time and means available, forced to decide which soldiers must be saved and which must die. Some jobs, with a little attention, can be kept alive until later. Others may be passed on to associates, and others are best deemed dead.
- By renegotiating deadlines; they are not written in stone
- By setting aside all the *trivialities* that we can for another day
- By implementing *alternative work plans*
- By delegating routine matters to someone else
- By reconsidering priorities. We avoid impulsive actions such as making unnecessary telephone calls, and we put out of sight all materials that might distract us. We might even hang up a sign saying something like, 'I am putting out a fire until . . .'
- By looking for help for key jobs
- By extending our field of vision: there is no use concentrating today when something goes wrong. Once it has happened, it will

be necessary to re-evaluate what has gone wrong and to consider why things built up; lessons are learnt from experience.

- And of course, most importantly, by deciding how we are going to fit this day into the *rest of our life*. In the context of our life, maybe it is not so important and stands out alongside many other days when things went like clockwork.

I hardly slept, I began with digestive problems and headaches. I wrongly turned to medicine instead of trying to change the circumstances or at least become more aware of them.

(human resources manager, father)

It has been shown that tensions and stress occur when we exceed the curve of well-being. This ranges from five and a half to eight hours of work per day. If we work less, perhaps much of our time lacks structure, which can also cause stress; if we work more, this may generate stress and tiredness. Unawares, we may also be deceiving ourselves and struggling for false family and professional self-realization when we have set objectives that are not very realistic or achievable.

Early symptoms of stress are nervousness (others see this immediately), mood swings (we are disturbed by 'wasting time' to go to the cinema with friends), intellectual difficulties (memory lapses), personal insecurity (apathy), mistrust (doubts about oneself and those around us).

In more acute phases, there is mental fatigue (inability to solve problems), hypersensitivity (we are disturbed by things that we had not noticed before), anxiety (at not being able to cover all the work), nervous pain, gastric disorders, breakdown in the hierarchy of values (we give importance to insignificant things).

The best way of reducing this, bearing in mind that stress is an automatic reaction to a state of overload, is by rationally facing up to the crises and resolving them, as the danger lies in turning a way of operating on chronic levels of tension into a habit. For some people, this situation is exhilarating; in fact they are the ones who create it: deadlines are tight, they always have to finish things in a hurry and they go constantly from crisis to crisis.

We are then faced with a similar situation to the one that occurs with dancers, actors and speakers who sometimes have the feeling of 'collapsing' at the end of the performance. These people have similar reactions when the rushing ends, when the quarterly report is finally finished, when the deal has been pinned down and nerves have calmed. In fact, this feeling indicates that the body is returning to its normal state after a time of crisis. These times of tranquillity must be used to organize one's ideas, to establish new targets and celebrate our achievements. It is also important to discover what are the most stressful factors for us and try to avoid them or deal with them appropriately.

The personal mission

As we were saying at the beginning of the chapter, managing time (given the fact that we live in the co-ordinates of time and space) entails managing our own life. Each person, each family and also each company has to discover its mission, what it was called for and the aspects in which it cannot be replaced, to be able to discover the role that it must play at all times. Only in this way, by realizing that our guiding light is not events but rather our mission, will we be capable of recognizing order under apparent chaos. Sometimes our life or other's lives may seem disorderly and chaotic, like the weather. However, there are laws guiding it; it has meaning and tendencies, although they are not obvious to everyone.

Running a company, running a home or 'simply' running our own lives are tasks that require above all a clear idea of our personal and professional mission. The mission is the mirror image of each person and must be revealed. It is unique and unrepeatable. It includes the things that only that person can do simply because they are that person, with their talents, abilities, predispositions, potential for development, previous decisions, current circumstances and personal history, which becomes activated through the different roles we play.

We therefore need to discover those facets which only we can carry out and where we are truly essential (the wives of our husbands, mothers or fathers of our children, sisters of our brothers, friends of our friends). Maybe we need to stop and reconsider from time to time what cannot be delegated, establishing principles and clarifying our priorities. However, this reflection must end up scheduling the 'moments of truth' in our diaries which may not be renounced to be true 'home builders'. Time spent together is necessary; a father's diary must include the whole of his life, and he must also be capable of finding family time with the same intensity with which he blocks off work time.

At a very young age, our children must also learn to manage their time (activities, studies) not only to their own benefit but also in order to have a full life that encourages greater socialization. Instead of providing large blank spaces, school diaries should suggest sections (studies, friends, family, sports, chores, volunteering) which would accustom them starting from childhood to building a full life.

Having identified our roles as individuals, spouses, parents, children, brothers and sisters, brothers-in-law and sisters-in-law, children-in-law, professionals, members of the community, country, party or religious denomination, we define our targets for each of them in the context of what is feasible, of what is possible. Then we will turn these into activities with a planned date and time. An essential instrument for achieving these targets is once again the diary. As we said before, its use is no more than a reflection of our system of priorities, and having a single diary (not one in our pockets, another in the office and another in the kitchen) is a way of helping our memory at all times. Then we must specify what the best times are (according to our biorhythms) for working on activities and tasks that bring us closer to our targets and, as far as possible, block out this time, saving spaces, especially, when we see a danger of professional life invading family life.

A diary does not only contain commitments imposed on us, appointments that others make or that we have made; it also contains the time we commit to ourselves to be able to develop this important professional career, as well as our family and personal life. We write in our diaries, blocking off times, but at the same time being flexible to new circumstances which might oblige us to change our plan. We therefore write in pencil, to avoid the frustrating situation of not having accomplished something:

> It's not a question of doing everything...but knowing how to prioritize. I have realized that only when I know this and I'm capable of resting in small spaces of time each day that my life gives me.
> (account executive in an advertising agency, three children)

A diary is thus in line with our real life and becomes the perfect back-up for our brain, because we are only one person. This might seem obvious, but it is not usual. Pareto's 80/20 Law reminds us that we should identify the activities that take up 20 per cent of our time and which, however, give us 80 per cent of the results and the self-realization in our life (and are therefore not delegable), and identify the activities that occupy 80 per cent of our time but only account for 20 per cent of the results and which, therefore, may be entrusted to another person:

> I try to spend most of my time on the few most important matters. Sometimes the time I spend on this is negligible. However, I have seen that things usually work well when we know how to delegate what is not important, even though it might be urgent. The temptation might arise from thinking that one is jeopardizing one's career, but I do not think this is true: it is necessary to do things seriously, but it is not necessary to take them seriously. I try not to forget that I am not married to my career, but to my wife.
>
> (Belgian businessman, father of five)

The fact is that what is urgent is not always most important. 'Dress me slowly because I'm in a hurry' is the folk wisdom take on this. In general terms, we can state that what is urgent is determined by life itself, which seems to go faster and faster due to the bombardment of daily events, but the most important thing is defined by our system of priorities. With these to co-ordinates, Covey (see Table 7.1) helps us to reflect on our reality.

If we concentrate on the first quadrant, we feel that we are in constant crisis, and this is because we do not spend time on quadrant II, before the important activities that are not yet urgent become urgent. Quadrant II is the one of realism and quality of life, yet it requires discipline and self-control. We need time not only to do things but also to recover and to be able to continue doing them: these are what Covey calls 'preventative activities' to be able to continue producing. Human beings are made up of both body and spirit; therefore, time must be spent on sports and resting one's body, to intellectual training and good reading. We are also social by nature; therefore, it is very necessary to devote time to building relations at work and at home, and this is not simply a question of effectiveness (although it is this, too), but because it is an essential condition for us to develop as whole people. We also need time to

Table 7.1 The seven habits of highly effective people

	Urgent	Not urgent
Important	*Activities I* Crisis Pressing problems Project whose deadlines are met	*Activities II* Preventative activities Building relations Recognizing new opportunities Planning recreation
Not important	*Activities III* Interruptions, some calls Mail, some reports Some meetings Immediate, pressing matters	*Activities IV* Trivialities, useless clutter Some letters Some telephone calls Time wastage Pleasant activities

Source: Covey, 1990 *The Seven Habits of Highly Effective People*, Chapter II, Private Victory, 3rd Habit: Establish the First-things-first Principles of Personal Administration Quadrant II (p. 191).

discover and develop new opportunities and to plan and schedule changes and re-create them, in other words, to anticipate and facilitate their execution. Quadrants III and IV may be delegated; they are this 80 per cent of activities that achieve only 20 per cent of our goals, and they are almost always time thieves that must be stopped.

Our attention must preferably be focused on the upper quadrants, thus managing what is not important (whether it is urgent or not) in a subsidiary manner. We will thus be capable of devoting ourselves to this 20 per cent of work that cannot be delegated and which will bring in 80 per cent of the achievement of our objectives:

> The weight of my daily responsibilities is such that the urgent and important matters take up my whole day; I do not have a minute for anything else. Sometimes I realize that I should spend time with people; I feel a bit like a robot.
>
> (manager, two children)

People absorbed by the first quadrant (urgent and important) in fact do nothing more than handle crises. Their function is similar to that of a *fireman*, and they thus spend their lives putting out fires. They might do it well, but this situation cannot be sustained for long and definitely not permanently. The very likely results are stress, exhaustion and lower efficiency:

> My criterion is always to be highly available. I do not know how to say no.
>
> (management secretary, one child)

Those who focus on the third quadrant (urgent and not important) are actually living in *self-deceit*. They spend a lot of time on trivialities, useless matters (e-mails, telephone calls, meetings). They may be greater crisis handlers, but in fact they are only capable of concentrating on the short-term and end up considering that targets and plans are not worthwhile in achieving personal or professional success. The absence of planning due to the fact that they have given up leads them to feel impotent, unable to control situations. They are like puppets of their surroundings with very fragile or broken relations, and they end up adopting a chameleon-like character, attentive above all to their reputation:

> I don't know whether I am to blame or whether it is my company's organization. I know that I waste my time on a thousand things which are undoubtedly activities, but I do not know where I am going. I don't know which are necessary for my work and which are simply a complement to my main activities.
>
> (publicist, single)

In the case of people in quadrants III and IV, this is where the greatest danger lies not only because of the fall in personal efficiency, but also due to the work and affective consequences. The combination of urgent and non-urgent matters, which are also not important, results in a *frivolous* personal make-up. Total irresponsibility arises in such cases; different employees are dismissed and there is ongoing dependence on others or on being governed by basic needs.

People centred in quadrant II (non-urgent and important activities) are *realistic*. They have vision, perspective, balance, few crises and greater quality of life. But to achieve this it is necessary to have a good dose of discipline and personal self-mastery. Investing time in this quadrant helps to prevent quadrant I from expanding with important matters that could become urgent.

It has taken me time to achieve it, but I have learnt to see things in the long term. For me, the core of the day is determined by what is truly important on all levels, personal, family, work, that day, whether it is urgent or not. This doesn't mean that I ignore everything else, but it means a great effort to prioritize. Such simple things like blocking off times in my diary to attend meetings with my children's teachers as if it was a meeting with one of my best customers, have for me become something more than a strategy; they have made me capable of really putting my children first.

(tax advisor, three children)

It is like the American Cecilia Royals, a mother of eight and President of the National Institute of Womanhood (NIW), says:

For me, a balance does not consist of finding the perfect midpoint between rival demands, rather knowing which demand needs my maximum attention, and when and what may be left unattended for a time. It consists of redirecting my efforts as many times as needed to achieve the end objective and learning to know that sooner or later I'll get there if it is important enough. It means ridding oneself of the obsession for personal prestige. Balance entails not losing sight of the objective, although it might seem you're going in the wrong direction. It is very similar to sailing against the wind.[2]

Learning to 'make a family'

I eat in half an hour, quite often a sandwich or a salad alongside the computer. I do this to get off early and spend more time with my family. Sometimes it is difficult to try to call off a meeting at 7 o'clock in the evening with the excuse of my children's school or doctor, but this is the only way to change the culture, even though it means they call you Super Daddy.

(public administration official, two children)

Spanish managers spend an average fifty-two hours a week at work, which means they work an average of more than ten hours a day. We should add five hours of commuting, five taking care of the home and shopping, eleven hours of personal care and leisure and four hours devoted to studies. Therefore, the family receives an average of seventeen hours a week. It is interesting to observe the influence on a family of parallel professional careers of both spouses, even more so when they are both managers. Women spend more time with their family than men, especially if the men have posts of great responsibility. If both are managers, the amount of time falls for both. And so we find more and more empty homes at crucial times of the day when the children need to talk and share what has happened to them at school.

Our world characterized by globalization, rushing and telecommunications; it requires greater maturity from us and for us to realize that having a family is not something purely material or formal, but that it requires wanting to be active home builders in the same way as we build our professionalism each day and end up having a career.

Given this situation, the first thing that has to be done is to deal with the individual realm. It is necessary to start with the *personal and marital unit to resolve the conflict*, bearing in mind that it will never be possible to give attention and quality time if there is not a minimal amount of time put in:

> You have to talk about everything and this, too. It is not a question of deciding what things each one will do in the home, but realizing that a home is a project that requires involvement. The hours put in are a symptom, but not the guarantee. Our professional diary must have time blocked out for the family and for meetings with the most important, decisive customer.
>
> (computer technician, two daughters)

Families have a mission that they alone must discover. First is mutual aid: the family is created by the efforts of all its members. Then we must ensure that this influence reaches other families as well as the community and society where we live. Therefore, we must clearly know what we want to do, where we want to go, and based on this define our roles inside and outside the home, identifying what may or may not be delegated in each case. Our actions reaffirm our convictions. Events often lead us towards a certain situation simply because we do not have the courage to decide. But for these decisions to make us better and truly build a home, they must reflect values, objectives and priorities guided by our personal and family mission, which is unique and unrepeatable, to which we are called because we are who we are and not others. As Robert Schuller said, 'You do not have a problem, but a decision to take.'[3]

On a personal level, just as in the professional realm, one must be capable of *taking decisions and being prepared to carry them out*. Only in this way can professionals and specific people be capable of partici-pating in both the family and work *with body and soul*, without psychological barriers, without blocks, with absolute dedication through quality time to each concern. In this way, *both realities, work and family, mutually benefit*.

In short, neither the self-sufficient strategy of a superwoman (rationalization of the conflict, strength of will and overload) nor that which avoids any overlap between the worlds, leading to a schizo-phrenic separation co-existing within an individual, is correct. Maybe the ideal model should give greater consideration to the complemen-tariness of the couple in all facets of life: work, family, society. The result will then be harmony partly attempted and premeditated on an individual level, but also the result of the joint will of the spouses, who do not avoid the problem but decide to approach it with a vision towards the future and to resolve it day-by-day.

Activity and reflection

> I get the feeling that I am being dragged along by events. I don't stop all day, but for me now it would be a dream to be able to plan. Maybe the disorder of my work has an influence on my home, or maybe it is the other way round.
>
> (fashion stylist, single)

Planning is limited to trying to reduce the uncertainties of the future as much as possible. It consists of *making forecasts* in order to achieve required objectives instead of simply limiting oneself to *reacting* to events or circumstances that arise. As a result, the person has a commitment to the decision taken.

Whereas planning is deciding what has to be done, scheduling is deciding when. This task requires flexibility so that important concerns and also anything unexpected may be covered. Depending on the kind of work, the time that unexpected events take up may vary significantly. Therefore, it is necessary to make realistic schedules in each case. A sales manager, for example, might leave 70 per cent of the day for unexpected events and can only block off two hours a day for what he has scheduled.

To ensure the success of both tasks, planning and scheduling, our objectives must be concrete, specific and therefore measurable, quantifiable and, to the extent possible, they must be few but important, compatible, attainable, but at the same time a little challenging and, of course, adapted for periods that can gradually be fulfilled through intermediate breaks that make it easier to meet them. They must be written and easily checked so that they are in accordance with one's personal evolution. Defining objectives is the same as giving direction to one's life. Priorities are closely related to long-term targets and are the basis of any plan.

So where is the trap? *Non-stop activity without intervals for reflection.* Although it is true that objectives are only attained through activity, through specific actions that make them come to fruition, we are capable of being so busy with what we are doing that we end up forgetting why we are doing them. Therefore, by establishing each activity's priority, we guarantee its efficacy and we ensure that in the event of anything unexpected arising, this priority will always be the essential decision-making factor.

It is thus explained by the United States executive Kirby Smith. In his case, there is clearer awareness that personal time, though scarce, is an essential space in his life to be able to recover from the efforts of work and family, to reflect as a matter of habit and avoid activism. This is the cornerstone to effective planning:

> I do not like to talk about a 'balance' between work and family, in fact we must be outstanding in both. What we do as parents is simply another kind of work. My colleagues laugh when they hear coffee coming out of the coffee machine at half past three in the afternoon. They understand that my second job, that of being a husband and father, is about to start, and that at times I need this extra dose of coffee to be able to be '100 per cent' when I go home each day. We cannot stand out in our work as parents if we do not arrive home punctually. While we are performing our professional responsibilities, we have to work quickly and constantly to be able to leave on time each day. A good diary, establishing priorities and a propensity for action are useful. In recent years, when my

profession required more time of me and a forty-hour working week was not sufficient, I learnt to value each minute of my day. I prefer to skip lunch or have a bite to eat at my desk than to miss my sacred dinner-time at 6 o'clock at home. With this dinner-time as my limit, I believe I have become a better professional, making better use of my time in the office and not wasting it.[4]

How to make our time at work more profitable

In addition to discovering how we spend or use our time, and using our diary (essential for a professional who is also a father or mother), we need a global vision, which is nothing other than the ability to transcend the present in order not to feel overwhelmed by it and be capable of pursuing objectives that might not have emerged today. Nurturing a global vision involves nothing more than:

Clarifying the valuable objectives in our life.
Having a satisfactory personal life that is balanced with our professional life.
Having well-defined targets.
Limiting the number of projects we take on depending on our priorities.
Laughing more frequently: taking everything seriously is not good for one's health.

A person who has a *global vision* is someone who masters his or her time:

- They have perspective; they put a distance between themselves and things
- They trust their imagination, which is creative or practises creativity
- They reflect; they think a lot; before doing anything, though only a minute, they think about what they are going to do
- They know themselves well or they strive to do so
- They use techniques or tools that enable them to improve their use of their time
- They are the masters of their activities and maintain their initiative over them
- They continuously seek a balance in all facets of their life

- They plan even though they know that often they will not go as far as they want
- They have a good associate who helps them organize themselves better
- They delegate and assume the risk of errors that they are undoubtedly going to commit
- They fight constantly against overstretching themselves and do not become discouraged, although sometimes they might be overstretched

They are also capable of maintaining *a high energy level*. How? They are guided by objectives, establishing clear purposes for the whole day, being *realistic*. (The time available is not the whole day, but only 50 per cent of 75 per cent, bearing in mind unexpected things that will require our attention. It is not necessary to schedule one's agenda for a 22-hour day.)

- They assign priorities to tasks; only when they know what they have to achieve do they establish priorities amongst pending matters
- They finish what they begin: many things begun at the same time distracts one's mind; something completed gives a *sense of achievement.*
- They have a good relationship with themselves; they stop a few minutes a day to rest, stroll, meditate or have a nap
- They realistically make a 'to do' list, leaving all trivial work for times when they do not have much energy; the worst things must be resolved first.

If this is the starting point, it is not difficult to take on the following *four necessary habits to make our work and our time more efficient.*

Designing and assessing tasks

I always do it at the beginning of a week, and sometimes more often. It helps me to have a view of all pending matters so it is easier to put them in order.

(teacher, three children)

If we also wish to improve our productivity, we must have system. The first measure, universally used and similar to the traditional housewife's shopping list, consists of nothing other than making a master 'to do' list. This includes noting down any idea, task assigned or to be assigned, phone call, project or errand that arises, regardless of its importance.

Once this becomes a habit, the normal thing is to check the list each day and divide the large projects into smaller portions. The daily list is drawn up each morning by selecting tasks from the master list. It is good to classify them (1, 2 or 3 ...) according to their priority and the effort they require. Never schedule more than three or four category one priorities each day, and spread the rest out between priorities two and three. Then try to evaluate the tasks on the daily list in terms of profitability. If we are also capable of determining our most productive time, even better. In this way we will be capable of carrying out non-priority tasks during the times of low activity. Another way to improve our time management by grouping the calls and appointments into time blocs as much as possible. Our brain will thank us for it.

Deciding and delegating

I have discovered that almost every time we do not decide it is through fear or because the subject is difficult to take on, not because we do not know the solution. With our children the same thing happens, with the added aggravation that sometimes we do not want to see what is happening. It is necessary to decide in good time and to apply the solutions in good time. The same thing happens at work. I have reached the conclusion that only people who decide are capable of delegating later. The method is the same: not to hold back matters, not to get blocked on subjects. One thing that helps me to decide and delegate is thinking that almost all blockages are mental. My father said that what is impossible becomes possible if you have the will and accept it. The same action is easier the sooner it is done.

(executive, pregnant)

We have all said at some time, 'I will decide tomorrow'. The important thing is to know why. For indecisive people, not very valid reasons are usually invoked for justifying one's behaviour: lack of information, perfectionism, the fear of being wrong. However, tomorrow comes and does not sort out the situation. In a manager, this *risk component* in the decision-making is inherent to their work, which consists of deciding, and nobody is going to do it for them. A board of directors may be consulted but rarely decides. A manager must accept that he or she must take decisions without sharing responsibility; therefore, it could be said that it is preferable to take an imperfect decision on time than a perfect decision too late.

One pseudo-problem is being unnecessarily concerned with 'white elephants' about which we may not be able to do anything today. It is even thought that it is impossible to enjoy life until we have dealt with them. This attitude is not realistic and only leads to frustration. New 'white elephants' always appear and we will have to decide how to deal with them.

Furthermore, managers, fathers and mothers all manage people, and not tasks; rather they manage processes by managing people. Therefore, managing is delegating, measuring, accompanying, correcting, educating:

> The children's household chores are a prime educational instrument, and not so much for the basic work they relieve us of as for the sense of responsibility that they develop.
>
> (managing director of a publishing house, mother of five)

The danger of not knowing, or not being capable of 'making do', is that everything accumulates in our hands, making others have to check with us on every move, and in the end we are incapable of taking the right decisions. Delegating functions, tasks and responsibilities to others is one of the most difficult things that a person must do and at the same time it is a clear sign of their personal and professional maturity. To achieve it, one must have a working method, order and rigour.

What should be delegated? In fact, everything that one of our associates or, at home, one of our children might do sufficiently well. The problem lies precisely here, in thinking that they will never be capable:

> I believe that the money invested [yes, invested not spent] on household help enables significant physical and psychological well-being for working mothers and therefore for the whole family. My husband and I prefer to go out to dinner modestly on

Fridays than to dine in a classy restaurant and spend the difference
on relieving ourselves of household work such as cleaning or ironing.
(managing director of a publishing house, mother of five)

Not 'paralysing' matters by leaving them stacked up on our desk and consequently in our heads as well

Any paperwork (real or on the computer) involves previously taking
one of these four decisions:

(1) Throw it away. Does this paper or e-mail have any value for me
now or in the future? If not – in the waste paper basket. Let us not
forget that *the waste paper basket is a tool of triumph.*
(2) Send it: to the secretary, to a colleague or to another person who
might be interested.
(3) Act on it: in the event that it needs a reply from us (letter, analysis, review).
(4) File it: distinguishing papers that might have a personal use or
interest in the future, always assigning an expiry date.

It is essential to master complex subjects, subjects that have been put
off or sent by means of the diary/pending matters filing system. We
can use 31-divider files for this, placing each paper in the numbered
compartment corresponding to the date when we want to work on it.

Making meetings functional

We live in a country that loves meetings, but we also have to recognize that most times they are not very productive. The key question is:
is the time that is going to be spent on this meeting worth the output
that is going to be achieved from it? Based on this, we can begin to be
more functional and keep asking ourselves: 'Am I clear on the objectives of this meeting?' 'Do I need advice from all of those who are
going to come?' 'Are so many points of view necessary?' 'Could the
matter be resolved with a representative from each department?' 'Is
the group's participation important for the problem that I'm going to
solve?' 'Do I need the group's vote to approve a new policy?' 'Will this
meeting be for decision-making or simply informative?'

Very often we realize that there are cheaper, faster or more comfortable
ways of getting the same results, such as, for example, sending a memo

to the team or setting out the matters in writing so that the staff might read them, reflect and absorb them or give their opinion, answering in writing, and even giving a deadline for it. If we are honest with ourselves, we will realize that many of the things for which meetings are called can be solved by telephone or e-mail. Once the benefits of holding the meeting has been decided, the objectives must be clearly set, and we must decide on whether we should call only the key personnel, that is, those who will contribute directly to achieving the objective, instead of others.

At least 24 hours before the meeting, the agenda should have been distributed to set out the objectives of the meeting, the matters to be dealt with, the decisions that have to be taken with respect to what, and the problems that have to be resolved in the time available to deal with each matter. After each meeting, there should be a written summary, the minutes, encompassing all agreements and decisions and those responsible so that it is clear who is going to do what and when. If these minimal requirements are not fulfilled, we are faced with fruitless, ineffective and frustrating 'meetingitis', which casts doubt on the competence of the person running them. Time is money for everyone.

To sum up and as a key idea in this chapter, it is important to state that managing our time is nothing more than managing our own life. Life is time, and the decisions we take on its use are a clear indication of where we want to go, of what direction our life is taking and of what we really want to do.

It would be useless to know the keys of effective organization and time management if we did not know where we were going, that is, if we had not discovered our unique, unrepeatable personal mission.

Having a clear view of our mission and the different roles in which it is to be deployed (personal, family, professional, social) involves activating our entire system of priorities and putting it into practice in specific, daily actions, such as blocking off times in our diary for the important activities in each of these areas.

Being born and living are not personal options, but living life to the fullest and being the masters of the years we have lived as if they were a fixed investment – this does lie within our abilities. Its yield and our happiness are only a question of willpower and clear ideas.

Notes

Introduction

1. A study made by the sociologist Catherine Hakim, published in 'Work-Lifestyle Choices in the 21st Century', *Britain Journal of Sociology*, vol. 49, issue 1, London School of Economics.
2. André Frossard, *God Exists, I Found Him*, Rialp, Madrid, 1965.

1 Being a Woman in the Twenty-first Century

1. Janne Haaland Matlry, *The Time of Women. Notes for a new feminism*, Rialp, Madrid, 2000.
2. D. Herlihy, 'Land, family and women in continental Europe 701–1200', *Traditio*, 1962.
3. R. Pernoud, *Women in the Time of Cathedrals*, Granica, Barcelona, 1982 (pp. 191–3).
4. Gloria Solé Romeo, *The History of Feminism*, Eunsa, Pamplona, Spain, 1995 (p. 43).
5. Herbert Marcuse, *Marxism and Feminism*, Jahrbuch Politik 6, Berlin, 1974 (p. 86).
6. In 1949 we saw the appearance of de Beauvoir's book *The Second Sex* ([Le Deuxième sexe], Gallimard, Paris, 1949). Twenty years later the author revised her own thesis in *The Broken Woman*, (Gallimard, Paris, 1963). In 1963, the American Betty Friedan wrote a bestseller, *The Feminine Mystique*, (Editorial Júcar, Gijón, 1974) which demanded the liberalization of abortion as a gateway to personal freedom.
7. Jutta Burggraf, 'In search of a new relationship between men and women', *Folleto Mundo Cristiano*, no. 495, 1989.
8. Julián Marías, *Women in the 20th Century*, Alianza Editorial, Madrid, 1981.
9. E. Badinter, *The Masculine Identity*, Alianza Editorial, Madrid, 1993.
10. Friedan, *The Feminine Mystique*.
11. Friedan, *The Fountain of Age*, Planeta, Barcelona, 1994.
12. Germaine Greer, *Sex and Destiny*, Plaza & Janés, Barcelona, 1985.
13. Jean Elshtain, *Public Man, Private Woman*, Princeton University Press, Princeton, 1981.
14. Virginia Held, 'Mothering versus contract', *Revista Atlántida*, issue 13, 1993.
15. Andrea Boachetti (Director of the Virginia Wolfo Centre in Rome), 'Neo-feminism. The conquest of being different', *Bathia*, 1985 (pp. 70–5).
16. Solé Romeo, *The History of Feminism* (p. 24).
17. L. Polo, 'The co-existence of man', in *Actas XXV Reuniones Filosóficas de la Facultad de Filosofía de la Universodad de Navarra*, Pamplona, 1991.

18. Cecilia Royals (President National Institute for Womanhood, USA), CD Rom, *Family-profession, a daily challenge*, IESE Publishing, 2002.
19. J. Ballesteros, *Postmodernity, Decadence or Resistance*, Tecnos, Madrid, 1989.
20. John Gray, *Men are from Mars, Women are from Venus*, Grijalbo Mondadori, Barcelona, 2001.
21. Carlota Barcino, 'Man: That enigma that complements me', Web: Mujer Nueva, 2003.
22. S. Poelmans, N. Chinchilla and I. Martí, *Decision Criteria in Selection Processes in Spain: Are Women Discriminated Against?*, a study conducted by IESE and the Fundación Addecco, 2003.
23. 'The rights of motherhood', *Nuestro Tiempo*, February 1998.
24. Christian Collange, *I Want to Go Back Home*, Grijalbo, Barcelona, 1968.
25. Gilles Lipovetsky, *The Third Woman*, Anagrama, Barcelona, 2002.
26. Betty Friedan, 'Twenty Years after The Feminine Mystique', *The New York Times Magazine*, 27 February 1983 (p. 56).
27. Victor Frankl, *Man's Search for Meaning*, Herder, Barcelona, 1999.
28. Blanca Castilla, *Male–Female Complementariness. New Hypotheses*, Rialp, Madrid, 1995.

2   The Family: Current Situation and Legal Framework

1. F. Fukuyama, *The Great Disruption: Human Nature and the Reconstitution of Social Order*, Free Press, New York, 1999.
2. Enrique Rojas, 'The Education of Desire', *Diario ABC*, 12 February 2003.
3. In the past year, the debt incurred by Spanish households increased by 14 per cent to a historical maximum of €448,282 million, due basically to the fall in interest rates, according to the Annual Report of the Bank of Spain.
4. Family responsibilities exclude 17.6 per cent of European women between 25 and 54 years of age from the labour market, according to a study prepared by Eurostat in 2003.
5. Eurostat, 2002.
6. Eurostat, 2000.
7. A speech by Professor Shirley Burgraff of the economics department of Florida A&M University (United States) in the 5th Oikos Nemo International Symposium organized by the University of Navarre.
8. Jean-Didier Lecaillon (economics professor at the University of Paris II Pantheon-Assas) in the 1st Congress of Large Families in Catalonia on 20 September 2003.
9. For example, in Croatia, women are entitled to 45 days of maternity leave before the expected birth date, which is extended to one year after the birth of the child. However, all women must take maternity leave of 28 days before the birth and six months after. In Denmark, women are obliged to take two weeks of maternity leave after the birth. In Italy, the law provides for a five-month maternity leave, which in some cases may be given to the father.

10. In Norway, maternity leave may be one year paid at 80 per cent of the salary, or 42 weeks paid at 100 per cent. This country has the highest birth rate in Europe next to Ireland (1.9 children per woman), and also one of the highest rates of female participation in working life in the world (67 per cent).

11. On the initiative of the Finnish government, a campaign has been launched to promote the role of the father, the keystone of which is the child's right to be brought up together with both of his or her parents. Likewise, in Cyprus there is an official programme attempting to achieve greater participation by men in family life and in relationships with the children.

12. In the Czech Republic, the working code has been amended with a view to achieving equality between men and women with respect to their family obligations.

13. The law on equal treatment of men and women.

14. The case of Norway, Germany and France, amongst others.

15. In Norway, paternity leave is used in 8 out of every 10 cases.

16. *El Mundo*, 11 June 2000.

17. *La Vanguardia*, 23 June 2003.

18. Amongst others, Belgium, Croatia, Cyprus, the Czech Republic, Denmark, Finland, France, Germany, Italy, Norway, Slovakia and the United Kingdom recognize this kind of leave, which is quite generous in countries such as Finland, Germany and Slovakia.

19. In Italy, parents are entitled to be absent from work for five days a year in order to deal with children over the age of three and less than five years old who are ill.

20. In Croatia, adoptive parents of children under 12 are entitled to take an adoption leave of 270 days counting from the date of the adoption, provided that the other member of the couple is not the biological parent of the minor. This entitlement has been envisioned for adopting couples, and this leave has also been recognized in France.

21. In Spain, there is a leave of absence to care for relatives, and in the case of children (either natural or adopted) it can be extended to a maximum of three years.

22. In Sweden, there is child-rearing insurance intended to allow parents to interrupt their professions for a period of at most 360 days to deal with bringing up their children. This insurance enables them to receive an income equivalent to 90 per cent of their usual salary.

23. The case of Cyprus, Ireland, Latvia and Portugal.

24. A study published by the Institute of Tax Studies (IEF) in June 2003.

25. Data taken from the study published by the Institute of Tax Studies (IEF) in June 2003.

26. Antonio A. Burgueño Torijano, *Preparing to Look After an Elderly Person: Seeking, Choosing and Assessing a Home*, Mira Editores, Zaragoza, 2002.

27. Cyprus, France, Norway, Slovenia, Spain.

28. Cyprus, France, Germany, Greece, Ireland, Latvia, Slovenia, Switzerland, United Kingdom.

29. Germany, Ireland, Lithuania.
30. Spain, Slovenia.
31. Greece.
32. Such as the mechanism started and financed by the government in Belgium. Similar formulae exist in Germany and Ireland.
33. A measure that appears, for instance, in the new working code of the Czech Republic.
34. Amongst others, the awards promoted by the federal government of Austria. Similar practices exist in Belgium and Germany.
35. For instance, the campaigns conducted in the United Kingdom.
36. A programme set up by the Irish government.
37. 'A comparative study of family policies in Europe', June 2003, unpublished presentation, presented at the First Conference for Large Families of Catalonia, 20 September 2003, available at www.europa.eu.int/comm/ employment_social/eoss/index_en.html
38. Starting in January 2004, the French state will pay €800 to pregnant women before birth in addition to a special supplement of up to €500 a month to the parent who gives up his or her job to look after the baby.

3   Women: Agents of Change?

1. Juan Antonio Pérez López and Nuria Chinchilla, *Woman and her Success*, Eunsa, 1999.
2. John Kenneth Galbraith, 'Corporate Man', *New York Times Magazine*, 22 January 1984.
3. Pilar García Lombardia, Pablo Cardona and Nuria Chinchilla, *The Most Highly Valued Management Competencies*, IESE Business School, working paper no. 01/4, November 2001.
4. Nuria Chinchilla and Consuelo León, *Female Values, More Humane Companies?*, IESE, March 2003.
5. A study conducted amongst the graduates of the IESE 2003 MBA programme.
6. Of all companies set up in Spain, more than half are created by women. They are generally SMEs with fewer than five employees. According to the Spanish National Institute of Statistics (INE), 47 per cent of companies without paid workers are managed by women, a percentage that rises to 55 per cent in commerce.
7. A study made by Bristol University and published in the *Sunday Times*, based on a sample of 1,100 people.
8. *The Working Profile of Spanish Women*, Whirlpool Foundation, 1995.
9. Dr Irene del Olmo, *Stress in Spain*, a study conducted for the Addecco Foundation, 1996.
10. National Health Survey, 2001.
11. Mary Anne Devanna, *Male/Female Careers. The First Decade*, Columbia University, Columbia, 1984 (p. 50).
12. *Opinion Data*, issue 10, January 1997.

13. Detailed analysis of the surveys of salary structure of the INE from 1993 to 1996 for the industrial and service sectors.
14. International Work Organization (IWO), 2003.
15. These data must be interpreted with care as under these figures there are significant differences in seniority in favour of men, and variable retribution also depends on the number of hours worked.
16. Data taken from a study sponsored by Ajax and the Ministry of Social Affairs, 2001.
17. The study, sponsored by SBC Communications Inc. and entitled *Women on the Boards of Directors of the 300 Largest Spanish Companies* concentrates on those with highest income. It was conducted for the Women's Global Summit (also called the 'Female Davos'), which took place in Barcelona in July 2002.
18. A study carried out by the Spanish trade unions CCOO and UGT for International Women's Day. March 2003.
19. Chinchilla and León, *Female Values, More Humane Companies?*
20. According to a 1987 survey carried out by the ILE network (Local Employment Initiatives) and the European Commission of more than fifty businesswomen in different countries, practically none of them exported. They had considered doing so but did not know how. A reflection on these results is contained in Nuria Chinchilla, Pilar García and Anna Mercadé, *Doing Business in the Feminine*, Ediciones Gestión 2000, Barcelona, 1999.
21. *Ibid.*
22. The author of the book *Dancing on the Glass Ceiling*, Contemporary Books, 2003.
23. A study conducted by Bristol University, 1999, quoted at www.Zenit.org
24. Lipovetsky, *The Third Woman.*
25. Carol Gilligan, *In a Different Voice: Psychological Theory and Woman's Development*, Harvard University Press, Cambridge, MA, 1982 (p. 29).
26. Daniel Goleman and Richard Boyatzis, *Resonant Leaders Create More*, Plaza y Janés, Barcelona, 2002. Daniel Goleman, *The Practice of Emotional Intelligence*, Kairós, Barcelona, 1999.
27. J.A. Pérez, *Women and their Success*, Eunsa, Pamplona, Spain, 1999 (p. 55).
28. Michael Korda, 'Emotions in a Woman's Briefcase', *SELF*, September 1983 (p. 60).
29. Pérez López and Chinchilla, *Woman and her Success* (p. 118).
30. Pérez López, *Women and their Success* (p. 28).

4 Work and Family: Can They be Reconciled?

1. Stewart D. Friedman and Jeffrey H. Greenhaus, *Work and Family – Allies or Enemies? What happens when business professionals confront life choices*, Oxford University Press, 2000 (pp. xv, 271).
2. Uma Sekaran, *Understanding the Dynamics of Culture in Networking: A Framework and an Initial Test*, Volume 5, JAI Press, Greenwich, CO, and London, 1990 (pp. 91–115).

3. J. Greenhaus and N. Beutell, 'Sources of conflict between work and family roles', *Academy of Management Review*, 1985.

4. N. Chinchilla and P. García, 'Die Familie – eine Schule der Kompetenzen', in Ch. Liepert, *Familie as Beruf: Arbeitsfeld der Zunkunft. Leske + Budrich*, Opladen, 2001 (pp. 197–205).

5. A term coined as a complement to strategic. Strategic skills look outside the company and the attraction of business. Intrategic looks inside the company and is concerned with the management of people (Cardona and Chinchilla: 'Evaluation and Development of Executive Capabilities', *Harvard-Deusto Business Review*, no. 89 (March–April 1999) 2000).

6. L.M. Verbrugge, 'Multiple Roles and Physical Health of Women and Men', *Journal of Health and Social Behaviour*, 24, University of Michigan, 1983 (pp. 16–30).

7. N. Chinchilla, S. Poelmans, S. Gallo and C. León, *Two Professions and One Family*, Department of Social Welfare and Family Affairs, Autonomous Government of Catalonia, July 2003.

8. Linda Waite and Evelyn Lehrer, 'Population and Development Review', www.Zenit.org, 27 September 2003.

9. N. Chinchilla, S. Poelmans, C. León, *Work-Family Conciliation Policies in 150 Spanish Companies*, IESE Research Document 498, March 2003.

10. Thirty-five is the age at which the greatest number of people are burnt out professionally, and the index of marriages ending up in divorce is on the rise.

11. Lotte Bailyn, *Breaking the Mould: Women, Men and Time in the New Corporate World*, Free Press, New York, 1993.

12. Chinchilla, Poelmans, Gallo and León, *Two Professions and One Family*.

5 Family-responsible Companies

1. In November 1999, a group of experts from the Massachusetts Institute of Technology signed a manifesto, 'What do we really want? A manifesto for the organizations of the 21st century', which talks of the integration of work and family as a step beyond conciliation, which forms part of the concept of a sustainable company.

2. S. Poelmans and N. Chinchilla, 'The Balance between Work and Family, a Concern for Spanish Companies?' FHN 330, May 2001. N. Chinchilla, S. Poelmans and C. León, *Work-Family Conciliation Policies in 150 Spanish Companies*. N. Chinchilla and C. León, *Best Practices of Company Work–Family Conciliation*, Autonomous Government of Catalonia, September 2003.

3. A participant with an interest in the company: suppliers, customers, employees, shareholders, local community, and so on.

4. Professor Jay Belsky, Director of the Institute for the Study of Children, Families and Social Issues at Birkbeck University (London).

5. www.Zenit.org, 5 April 2003.

6. *Sydney Morning Herald*, 21 March 2003.

7. According to a survey performed by the Foundation of Help for Drug Addiction (FAD) among 1,000 families with children between 14 and

20 years of age, 40 per cent of parents recognize that they do not deal well with conflicts arising in the family. Another study published by the US *National Review On-line* reveals that between 40 and 60 per cent of divorced couples wished they had worked harder to save their marriage.

8. In Spain, only 18 per cent of companies help in achieving this conciliation through their own nurseries or by giving their employees aid to pay for them. The Ministry of Employment and Social Affairs has encouraged a 'new' nursery plan for which it provides one-third of the budget (another third is paid by the companies and the rest is paid by the autonomous communities or town halls). According to official data, the amounts assigned to the communities for programmes for infant care and conciliation of family and working life (nurseries for children up to three years old) have increased by 60 per cent in the past four years.

6 The Secret of Personal Leadership

1. Daniel Goleman, *Emotional Intelligence*, Paidos, Barcelona, 1994.
2. S. Covey, *The Seven Habits of Highly Effective People*, Paidós, Empresa, 1990.
3. Chinchilla, Poelmans, Gallo and León, *Two Professions and One Family*.
4. Covey, *The Seven Habits of Highly Effective People*.
5. J.A. Pérez López, *Foundations of Company Management*, Rialp, Madrid, 1993.
6. Susana Tamaro, *Follow your Heart*, Seix Barral, Barcelona, 1994.
7. Gregorio Marañón, *The Count-Duke of Olivares or the Passion for Ordering*, Espasa-Calpe, Madrid, 1936.
8. Ricardo Yepes Stork, *Understanding Today's World*, Rialp, Madrid, 1993 (p. 159).
9. Julián Marías, *Human Happiness*, Alianza Editorial, Madrid, 1987.
10. Hermann Simon, *Leaders in the Shadows*, Planeta, 1997 (p. 267 ff.).

7 Managing Personal, Family and Professional Time: How to Accomplish Everything

1. P. Drucker, *The Practice of Management*, Heinemann Professional Publishing, London, 1989.
2. CD-Rom, *Family and Profession, A Daily Challenge*, IESE Publishing, 2002.
3. Robert Schuller is an American tele-evangelist. This is an expression often used by him.
4. CD-Rom, *Family and Profession, a Daily Challenge*.

Index

DATE DUE

GAYLORD | | | PRINTED IN U.S.A.